Commanding the Red Army's
Sherman Tanks

Commanding the Red Army's Sherman Tanks

The World War II
Memoirs of
Hero of the Soviet Union
Dmitriy Loza

Edited and translated by
James F. Gebhardt

University
of Nebraska Press
Lincoln & London

© 1996 by the University of Nebraska Press
All rights reserved
Manufactured in the United States of America

⊚ The paper in this book meets the minimum requirements
of American National Standard for Information Sciences—
Permanence of Paper for Printed Library Materials, ANSI
Z39.48-1984.

Library of Congress Cataloging-in-Publication Data
Loza, D. F. (Dmitriĭ Fedorovich)
Commanding the Red Army's Sherman tanks: the World War II
memoirs of Hero of the Soviet Union Dmitriy Loza / edited and
translated by James F. Gebhardt.
p. cm.
Based on unpublished ms. Skaz o tankakh "Sherman".
Includes bibliographical references and index.
ISBN 0-8032-2920-8
1. Loza, D. F. (Dmitriĭ Fedorovich) 2. World War, 1939–1945—Tank
warfare. 3. Sherman tank. 4. World War, 1939–1945—Personal
narratives, Russian. 5. Soviet Union. Raboche-Krest ianskaia
Krasnaia Armiia—Biography. 6. Soldiers—Soviet Union—
Biography.
I. Gebhardt, James F., 1948– . II. Title.
D793.L68 1997
940.54'8147—dc20
96-7366
CIP

Contents

Illustrations

Photos

Following page 56

The author in Hungary, March 1945, at the rank of Guards Captain

Captain Nikolay Maslyukov, commander of the 1st Battalion

Shermans of the 1st Battalion, 46th Guards Tank Brigade, Vienna, April 1945

A mortar crew deploys forward in Vienna under guard of a Sherman tank

An American-manufactured scout car advances with infantry, Vienna

A Sherman tank and an American-manufactured truck after the battle, Vienna

Guards Captain D. F. Loza and his father, Private Fedor Loza

Guards Senior Lieutenant Dmitriy Niyakiy

Guards Captain N. Bogdanov and Guards Lieutenant Mikhail Golubev

A Sherman makes its way across a causeway reinforced by cut logs

The Sherman in standing water

A Sherman that has just forded a stream

Maps

About the Author

Dmitriy Fedorovich Loza was born on 14 April 1922 in the village of Kolesnikovka, in the Shevchenkovskiy region of Kharkov oblast, to a Ukrainian peasant family. After completing high school, he entered the Soviet Army in 1940, and he graduated from Saratov Armor School in 1942.

Loza fought with Soviet forces against both Germany and Japan in World War II and on 15 May 1946 was awarded the USSR's highest decoration for valor, Hero of the Soviet Union, for his actions in the battle for Vienna, Austria. He graduated from the Frunze Academy (the Soviet equivalent of the U.S. Army Command and General Staff College) in 1956 and served as an instructor there before retiring in 1967 at the rank of colonel.

Loza subsequently was a senior researcher and lecturer at a Moscow institute, authoring and coauthoring four books: *Marsh i vstrechnyy boy* [The march and meeting engagement] (Moscow: Voyenizdat, 1968), *Preziraya smert'* [I scorn death] (Moscow: DOSAAF, 1970), *Motostrelkovyy batal'on v boyu* [The motorized rifle battalion in combat] (Moscow: Voyenizdat, 1972), and *Taktika v boyevykh primerakh* [Tactics in combat examples] (Moscow: Voyenizdat, 1974). He received the prestigious Frunze Prize in 1982 for his contribution to this last work. In addition to Hero of the Soviet Union, his decorations include the Order of Lenin, the Order of the Red Banner, the Order of Alexander Nevskiy, the Order of the Patriotic War (1st and 2d degree), two Orders of the Red Star, and several other medals.[1]

About the Translator

James F. Gebhardt, a native of North Dakota, enlisted in the U.S. Army in 1966 and served three years as an infantryman, including one tour in the Republic of Vietnam. He was commissioned in armor branch through ROTC at the University of Idaho in 1974, where he graduated with a Bachelor of Arts in political science, and earned a Master of Arts in history at the University of Washington in 1976. In 1983, after commanding a tank company in Germany, Gebhardt entered the Soviet Foreign Area Officer program, studying Russian at the Defense Language Institute in Monterey, California, and the U.S. Army Russian Institute in Garmisch, Germany. Major Gebhardt served successively as a history instructor at the Command and General Staff College and analyst at the Soviet Army Studies Office, both at Fort Leavenworth, and as an escort officer and deputy field office chief for the On-Site Inspection Agency at Travis Air Force Base, California, before retiring in 1992. He is the author of *Leavenworth Papers No. 17, The Petsamo-Kirkenes Operation: Soviet Breakthrough and Pursuit in the Arctic, October 1944* (Fort Leavenworth KS: U.S. Army Command and General Staff College, 1990), and the translator of *Blood on the Shores: Soviet Naval Commandos in World War II,* by Twice Hero of the Soviet Union Viktor Leonov (Annapolis MD: Naval Institute Press, 1993; also published in paperback under the title *Blood on the Shores: Soviet SEALs in World War II* by Ivy Books, 1994). He has written numerous articles for professional military journals. He currently resides in Leavenworth, Kansas, and works at Fort Leavenworth for a defense contractor.

Translator's Introduction

       Anyone with more than a passing interest in World War II knows that the U.S. government supplied military equipment to many of its allies, including the Soviet Union, through the Lend-Lease program.[1] The Soviets received this matériel by sea through Murmansk and Arkhangelsk in the far north, Vladivostok and Magadan in the Far East, and Persian ports in the Middle East. About half of the approximately fourteen thousand aircraft were delivered disassembled on the decks and in the holds of ships, and the other half were flown via Alaska and across the Bering Strait or over the south Atlantic Ocean and Africa.

       Although the Soviet historiography of World War II does not ignore the contribution of American military equipment to the Soviet Union's war effort against the German and Japanese armies, it tends to minimize it. Postwar Soviet official histories generally reflect the line expressed in the *Soviet Military Encyclopedia:* that the total goods and matériel shipped to the Soviet Union during World War II did not exceed 4 percent of Soviet domestic production.[2] Postwar Soviet official accounts contain fairly accurate quantitative indicators of Lend-Lease deliveries during the war but often denigrate the quality of American equipment or fail to characterize its contribution to the war effort. Only since the collapse of the Soviet Union has this historiographical trend begun to shift, and now a Soviet author has even suggested that "without the Western supplies, the Soviet Union not only could not have won the Great Patriotic War, but even could not have resisted German aggression."[3]

       Soviet memoirs and war fiction frequently contain references to *Dakota* (c-47 Skytrain or Dakota transports), *Kobra* and *King Kobra* (p-39 and p-63 pursuit planes), and *Boston* (a-20 twin-engined attack bombers) aircraft, and the *Villis* (Willys jeep) and *Studebeker* (Studebaker truck). These and other mentions of American military equipment, and also clothing and food, are generally presented in a positive context but without elaboration.

In the twenty years that I have followed this topic, Dmitriy Loza's first-person account is the most detailed description I have seen of the employment of U.S. military equipment by the Red Army. The subject of his account is the M4A2 Sherman Medium Tank, powered by a General Motors twin-diesel (two six-cylinder truck engines mounted together) and armed with a 76-mm main gun.[4] His story is a collection of anecdotes that speak to the life of a junior Red Army tank officer at the small-unit level. Some are humorous, others will put a lump in the reader's throat. But all will make us proud of the contribution made by American equipment to the war in the East.

The Soviets received approximately twelve hundred light and five thousand medium tanks from the United States during World War II. The first tanks shipped to the Soviet Union in 1941–42 were the M3A1 General Lee and the M3A5 General Grant, equipped with gasoline-powered engines. Stalin complained openly to Roosevelt about these early American tanks in his personal correspondence, writing, "U.S. tanks catch fire very easily when hit from behind or from the side."[5] The Americans responded by ceasing delivery of gasoline-powered tanks and sending instead the diesel-powered M4A2. Although in many ways the M4A2 was not equal in mobility to the Soviet T-34 or in firepower to the more heavily armed German tanks it faced, Red Army tank crews were able to employ it effectively in combat.

The Red Army organized its American tanks into units of three three-tank platoons per company, with a single tank in the company headquarters (ten tanks total), the company commanded by a senior lieutenant (starshiy leytenant, the equivalent of a first lieutenant in the U.S. Army). A tank battalion consisted of two tank companies with a battalion headquarters (twenty-one tanks total), commanded by a captain. A tank brigade, which consisted of two tank battalions (forty-two tanks) plus the brigade headquarters, was commanded by a lieutenant colonel. Tank brigades could exist as separate units or be joined together into a tank corps. Corps were generally subordinated to armies.[6]

The battalion to which Dmitriy Loza was assigned belonged to the 233d Tank Brigade of the 5th Mechanized Corps. In September 1944, these units were redesignated 46th Guards Tank Brigade and 9th Guards Mechanized Corps respectively, the honorific titles attesting to their combat achievements.[7] Although it appears that the entire corps to which Loza's battalion belonged was equipped with Shermans, the other corps of the army was equipped with Soviet T-34 tanks.[8]

The story of how this material came to light is compelling. Retired Soviet Army officer and World War II veteran Dmitriy Loza hand-delivered his typewritten manuscript to the U.S. Embassy in Moscow in February 1994. Lieutenant Colonel (now Colonel) Ilona Kwiecien, the assistant U.S. Army attaché, passed the material to Lieutenant Colonel Timothy Thomas (U.S. Army, Retired), a mutual acquaintance of Colonel Kwiecien's and mine, who at that moment was in Moscow on temporary duty from the Foreign Military Studies Office at Fort Leavenworth. Aware of my interest in any materials pertaining to Lend-Lease to the Soviet Union during World War II, Tim brought Loza's manuscript back to Fort Leavenworth and handed it to me.

The original manuscript contained only a few explanatory footnotes, which I have identified by insertion of the letters DL. All other notes were inserted by the translator to amplify or clarify passages of text.

In addition to those persons mentioned above, I wish to acknowledge the contributions of many other colleagues in bringing this material to publication. Randy R. Love, of the Foreign Military Studies Office at Fort Leavenworth, provided timely and valuable assistance with passages of problematic Russian text. Lieutenant Colonel Anthony J. Bowers, U.S. Army (Retired), read and commented on the draft translation. Peter Maslowski, University of Nebraska, recommended it to the editorial board for publication. Colonel David M. Glantz, U.S. Army (Retired), also supported the publication of this material as a referee. Colonel Dmitriy F. Loza (Soviet Army, Retired) provided invaluable support from distant Moscow in securing permission to use photographs and in supplying additional textual material to bolster the original manuscript.

It has been both a delight and a personal honor to translate *Commanding the Red Army's Sherman Tanks*.

JAMES F. GEBHARDT
Leavenworth, Kansas

Author's Introduction

It is generally known that during the years of the Great Patriotic War, the Allies of the anti-Hitler coalition delivered a variety of combat equipment to the Soviet Union through the Lend-Lease program.

I was one of those predestined by fate to become a foreign-vehicle tanker[1]—to fight on the American Sherman M4A2 tank for almost two years. The crews affectionately named it the *Emcha* from the first letter and number of its alpha-numeric designation [M-4 in Russian is *M-chetyrye*].

There can hardly be found another item of foreign combat equipment that experienced such severe testing by the incredible dirt of the pulverized and obliterated front-line roads, the summer heat, the serpentine pathways and mountain passes of the Transylvanian Alps and southern reaches of the Grand Khinghan Range, and the scorched quicksands of the Gobi Desert. In the flat expanses of Manchuria, the Sherman literally swam across limitless bodies of water. Tropical August downpours, to which were added the contents of reservoirs emptied by the Japanese, had turned the ground into an immense sea. The tanks were forced to move hundreds of kilometers along railroad track embankments (on the cross ties).

The Shermans' armor felt the blows of the projectiles of German antitank guns, *panzerfausts*, and the main gun rounds of Tiger and Panther tanks.[2] Sherman tanks were subjected to German air strikes and even withstood encounters with Japanese kamikaze air attacks. The Emcha raced like a whirlwind across minefields, was blown up on fougasse obstacles, and burned with fire. In sum, these tanks and their crews experienced it all.

The brigades of the 5th Mechanized Corps were equipped with Sherman tanks beginning in mid-1943. This corps participated in the Korsun-Shevchenkovskiy, Jassy-Kishinev, Budapest, Vienna, and Prague offensive operations. As part of the Transbaikal *Front*, the corps defeated units and large formations of the Kwantung

Army in August–September 1945.[3] This, briefly, is the combat path of my corps. As we will see, the geography of the employment of Shermans was exceptionally diverse and the natural conditions quite varied.

The honorific title "guards," two honorary designations ("Dnester" and "Romanian"), and two decorations on its corps flag are recognition of the contribution of the corps' tankers, infantrymen, and artillerymen in tough battles in the West and Far East. Fifteen of these tankers became Heroes of the Soviet Union, and three became full holders of the Order of Glory.[4]

I had the fortune to combat German forces as part of the 233d (from September 1944, 46th Guards) Tank Brigade, 5th (9th Guards) Mechanized Corps, in the positions of chief of staff, deputy commander, and commander of a tank battalion. I fought on five different Shermans: two burned and three were seriously damaged in battle.

This work is not a description of the operations mentioned earlier. On these pages, I have attempted to portray the combat employment of a tank somewhat unusual for the Soviet Army, bringing to light its favorable and negative qualities (as compared to our T-34). I have written a word or two about the heroism of the Soviet Sherman crews. In all of this, I believe, I have made my modest contribution to filling in one of the "blank pages" of the history of the Great Patriotic War. Up to this time, there has hardly been a word printed in Soviet books, journals, and newspapers about the employment of British and American combat equipment on the fields of combat in World War II. Can this be fair?

PART 1

In the West

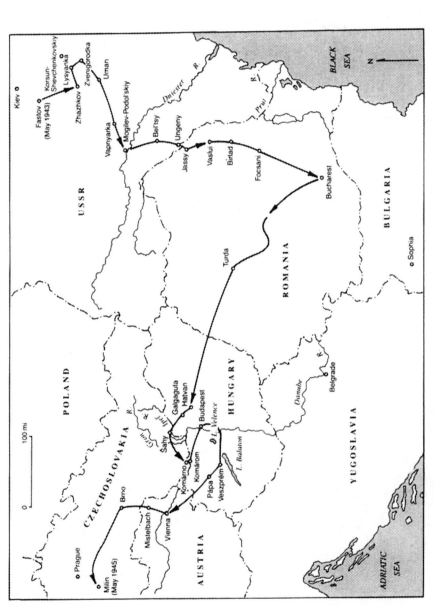

1 Combat path of the 46th Guards Tank Brigade. Eastern Europe. November 1943–May 1945.

The First Difficult Trials

Nineteen forty-three. The largest battle of World War II thundered on at Kursk in July and August. By November, the enemy had been thrown back to the right-bank Ukraine.[1] With each day, the front line inexorably receded westward. Germany and its satellites were forced to go over to the defensive. Occasionally, the enemy made vain attempts to retake the strategic initiative from the hands of the Red Army.

Thus, at the end of November and the beginning of December, the German command launched a powerful attack northward from the area south of Belaya Tserkov [eighty kilometers south of Kiev], with the intent to liquidate the Soviet forces' bridgehead on the west bank of the Dnieper River. Although hurriedly occupying defensive positions, our infantry forces were unable to withstand the powerful enemy thrust. The German attack threatened Belaya Tserkov, the capture of which would put them on the near approaches to Kiev, the Ukrainian capital.

Units of the 5th Mechanized Corps were in their second month of reconstitution in the forests north and west of Narofominsk [sixty-five kilometers southwest of Moscow]. Seven hours were set aside each day for rest, and the remaining time was spent in study of the equipment, gunnery at a range complex, and tactical field exercises. The following method was employed in our 233d Brigade to accelerate the mastery of the equipment. Permission was given to one crew in each battalion to disassemble almost completely one Sherman tank. The design and function of each instrument, component, system, and the armaments were studied. We had the full opportunity, as they say, to put our hands on a piece of "live" equipment. Ten days were spent in this exercise, after which the tank was reassembled by its crew. The deputy battalion commander for maintenance, together with the chief mechanic, monitored the assembly process, and the battalion armorer inspected the main gun and machine guns. A new group of "students" arrived and studied the "American" by the

3

same method. Detailed posters on the design and function of all the Sherman's systems and armaments had been issued in early October, and a good study guide had been published. Previous training methods were quickly abandoned.

Our training was interrupted on 15 November. An order was issued: during the night, the 233d Brigade's units were to rail-load at Narofominsk station and depart. To where? Only certain members high up in the chain of command knew the destination. By morning's first light, two of the brigade's first echelons [an echelon was one train] were on their way.

We experienced tankers understood: if tanks were being moved about by rail during the daylight hours, it meant that something bad was happening up at the front. By midday on 16 November, it became clear: we were going to Kiev. The train passed through one station after another, stopping briefly to change locomotives and allow the troops to be fed.

A day later, Kiev was behind us. We learned that the brigade would detrain at Fastov [sixty kilometers southwest of Kiev]. The lead echelon stopped suddenly in an empty field. A liaison officer from the staff of Second Ukrainian *Front* handed [brigade commander] Lieutenant Colonel Nikolay Chernushevich written instructions and a map containing our combat mission: quickly detrain and, after conducting a road march, occupy defensive positions north of Fastov.[2]

It is easy to say, "Offload the tanks!" But how was this to be accomplished without any loading platform? Our first obstacle. And after this, another obstacle, no less troubling. The Sherman turned by using both differentials.[3] This tank could not easily turn "on a dime," to rotate 90 or 180 degrees, not a problem for the Soviet T-34. The American tank required a significant area to turn around. How could this be accomplished on a flatcar? The *front* staff representative was in a hurry to get us offloaded. Apparently, the situation at the front demanded the immediate introduction of fresh reserves.

The brigade commander immediately called a conference. He familiarized those present with the contents of the order he had received and requested the battalion officers to express their thoughts on the offloading issue. The 1st Battalion commander, Captain Nikolay Maslyukov, reported that his chief mechanic,

Senior Sergeant Grigoriy Nesterov, had offloaded tanks in a similar situation. He agreed to demonstrate how to "jump down off the flatcar" to the driver-mechanics and tank commanders.[4] The trail flatcar was pushed back several meters and stopped at a point where the distance to the ground was not more than a meter. The side was dropped. The driver-mechanic started the Emcha's motor, and "danced in place" with several somewhat risky forward and backward movements. It seemed that the iron monster would fall off the flatcar, but at the last instant the brakes held the machine tightly. Several agonizing minutes passed. Finally, the Sherman stood crosswise on the flatcar. It slowly moved forward, its nose suspended in air for a second, and then, a heavy thud. The planking groaned and popped, the metal sides of the flatcar squealed in protest. The tracks struck the ground heavily. Ballast from the roadbed and clumps of chernozem [black earth] flew in all directions. The motors raced and the Sherman lurched forward to level ground some fifteen meters from the tracks. The engines shut down. The head of Grigoriy Nesterov, the driver-mechanic, popped out of the driver's hatch, a broad smile on his sweat-covered face. The senior sergeant inspected the tracks and found them undamaged. The demonstration was completed with outstanding results.

Having observed this event, Lieutenant Colonel Chernushevich approvingly declared, "Circus artiste! A genuine virtuoso!"

The string of flatcars was broken down and staged at various locations where the crews had found suitable "trampolines" for driving their tanks off the flatcars. Ten minutes later, the powerful growl of motors, the crackling of splintering wood, and the noise of scraping metal hung over the steppe. Tank offloading was proceeding at full speed. Happy shouts rang out when a Sherman successfully "stepped off" onto the ground. And there were unhappy groans, as well. Two tanks lay on their sides. Several driver-mechanics massaged their swollen noses. The ill-fated tankers bustled about their "reclining" Emchas. Tanks coming from the flatcars quickly gathered around. They hooked onto the "lazy bones" with tow cables and righted them. The deputy battalion commander for maintenance, Senior Lieutenant Aleksandr Dubitskiy, and the driver-mechanics inspected all the components in the engine and crew compartments of the tipovers. There was no damage. The Shermans had withstood their trial by sudden collision. Fisher Body, Buick, Ford, and Chrysler had done their work well!

Two hours later, the brigade's battalions were ready for movement. The mutilated and abandoned flatcars stood on the tracks. After our field expedient offloading, they awaited a visit to the blast furnace.

Every journey begins with the first step. These steps were difficult. The autumn of 1943 was unusual in Ukraine: at night—a moderate frost, during the day—an occasional wet snow, and then rain. The roads were covered with a hard frozen crust during darkness that did not melt until midday. The Emchas had encountered a sort of skating rink. Each kilometer of the march route demanded great effort on the part of the driver-mechanics. The Sherman's tracks were rubber shoed to increase their service life and also to reduce the noise of their movement. There was practically no clanking of track, which was a trademark of the T-34. In these complex icy road conditions, the well-dressed tracks of the Sherman became its principal deficiency. It was as though the tanks were on skis.

The 1st Battalion moved out in the lead. Although the situation called for rapid movement, our speed was dramatically reduced. Whenever the driver-mechanic stepped on the gas, the tank became difficult to control. Even some of the experienced driver-mechanics ended up in the ditch or crosswise on the road. During the course of this "foxtrot" road march, it was confirmed that bad news does not travel alone. It quickly became clear that the Shermans were not only "easy sliders" but also "quick overturners." One of the tanks, having slid on an ice-covered road, threw a track to the inside on a small rise on the road shoulder and quickly laid over on its side.[5] The mouths of many tankers fell open in surprise. It was amazing to some. Our resident comic, Nikolay Bogdanov, maneuvering around the overturned Sherman, muttered sarcastically, "Fate smiles at us. From here on in, we own this beast."

What was the cause? Why did the Emcha turn over so quickly? What did we have to do to prevent this from happening in the future, to protect ourselves from injury? How could we stop the tank from sliding and, as the tankers said, not go "belly up"? Many tank commanders and driver-mechanics instinctively felt that the first cause of the disaster was the rubber-shoed track. They began to modify it by installing makeshift cleats. They twisted barbed wire on the outside edges of the track and installed bolts in the openings of the track blocks. The results were immediate. Our march speed increased sharply, and the journey was completed without further adventure. The brigade occupied a position three kilometers north of Fastov astride the highway leading to Byshev.

Days passed. The situation on the Kiev axis normalized. The forces defending the forward area stopped the enemy's offensive.

Brigade and battalion maintenance units began urgently to install cleats on the tracks (at any moment, an order might come down to road march to another position). In two hours, the Shermans had been "reshoed." Explanations were provided to all the tank commanders, driver-mechanics, and their assistants. There were three basic reasons for the Emcha's instability. The tank had significant height (3.14 m [10 ft., 4 in.]), a modest width (2.64 m [8 ft., 7 in.]), and a high center of gravity. This unfavorable ratio of closely related characteristics made the Sherman relatively unstable. Such somersaults did not occur with the T-34. It was lower than the American tank by 44 cm [17 in.] and wider by 36 cm [14 in.]. Its center of gravity was much more favorably placed.

I want immediately to say a good word about the manufacturer of the Shermans. Their representative was continuously available at the headquarters of the 5th Mechanized Corps. He scrupulously collected and studied all incident reports pertaining to the Emcha during its fielding, and through his own channels he reported them to the management of the appropriate companies. I can't recall his last name. It was categorically forbidden to conduct any kind of note-taking on the front line. But I remember we all called him Misha. Even now, at veterans' gatherings, we fondly recall how Misha, having observed a driver-mechanic attempting to twist something in the engine compartment, for example, with a key or a screwdriver, sternly spoke up: "This is factory sealed—tinkering is not permitted!" And the would-be tinkerer immediately lost the urge to turn and tighten screws. The Emchisti [Emcha tankers] later became convinced that these machines worked like a good chronometer with just normal maintenance resources.

Misha was quite distressed, even at times greatly depressed, that the Sherman demonstrated such poor maneuverability characteristics. He could not quietly look on at the efforts to improve the handling qualities of his firm's "baby." It was as though the arc welder had burned him personally.

Jumping ahead, I will remark that sometime in February of 1944, a complement of new tanks arrived in the brigade. In each tank's kit of spare instruments, lamp bulbs, and fuses were fourteen spare track blocks, factory-equipped with cleats. Thus the deficiencies of the tank's track had been quickly eliminated.

Rain, Snow, and Mud

The Korsun-Shevchenkovskiy operation (24 January–17 February 1944) was conducted by the forces of two *fronts:* First Ukrainian *Front,* commanded by Army General N. F. Vatutin, and Second Ukrainian *Front,* commanded by Army General I. S. Konev. The goal of the operation was to encircle and destroy a group of enemy forces consisting of the 1st Panzer and 8th Armies of Army Group South in the Korsun-Shevchenkovskiy bulge.

Powerful strike forces of both *fronts,* concentrated at the base of the bulge, carried out attacks from converging axes and joined in the area of the city of Zvenigorodka. Nine enemy infantry and one panzer division, along with a motorized brigade, were caught in the pocket. External and internal encirclement lines were established by 3 February 1944.

One of the particular features of this operation was that it was conducted in exceptionally complex weather conditions. At the start of the operation, Ukraine was experiencing an unusually warm winter. Rain or wet snow fell frequently during the day. At night, the temperature dropped to 25–28° F. The chernozem soil became so sticky that only tanks could move through it. The delivery of ammunition, fuel, and rations became extremely difficult. The troops were forced to employ horse, ox, and cattle teams to pull sledges. The local population, which had just recently been liberated from the Germans, carried shells, mines, and small arms ammunition by hand from one settlement to the next, where they placed this valuable cargo into the hands of others. This relay extended to the most forward positions. Aircraft delivered fuel for the tank armies.

The just-formed 6th Tank Army, consisting of the 5th Guards Tank and 5th Mechanized Corps, belonged to the First Ukrainian *Front*. The 5th Guards Tank Army belonged to the Second Ukrainian *Front*.

The forces of the Second Ukrainian *Front* went over to the offensive on 24 January 1944 and of the First Ukrainian *Front* on 26 January. The shock groups of the *fronts* (the tank armies) surged toward each other—toward Zvenigorodka. The enemy launched fierce counterattacks on 27 January against the flanks of the attacking Soviet forces, attempting to liquidate the penetration. Artillery and tank formations of the *fronts*, with the support of aviation, beat back the enemy's counterattacks. On 28 January 1944, the shock groups of both *fronts* joined together in the Zvenigorodka area, having accomplished the encirclement of the enemy's Korsun-Shevchenkovskiy grouping. The German fascist command was forced to curtail their counterattacks against the forces of First Ukrainian *Front* east of Vinnitsa and north of Uman to redirect all panzer divisions to the rescue of the encircled forces.

The second distinctive feature of the Korsun-Shevchenkovskiy operation was the employment of tank armies not only for rapid encirclement of the enemy but also to create the outer encirclement ring in the shortest time (by 2 March 1944). In the conditions of heavy mud, tanks were able to maneuver to the specified lines of defense. The tank armies of both *fronts* (5th Guards Tank Army and 6th Tank Army) were reinforced by infantry formations, antitank artillery, and engineer sapper units. While the tank armies were forming the outer encirclement ring, combined arms armies were forming the inner encirclement ring.

I was an active participant in the Korsun-Shevchenkovskiy operation. After recuperation in a hospital in November 1943, I was appointed chief of armaments of the 1st Battalion, 233d Tank Brigade.

After the linkup of the tank armies of the two *fronts* in Zvenigorodka, our 6th Tank Army received the mission quickly to conduct a night march to the west to occupy a defensive position on the outer encirclement ring. Never before or after this occasion did I witness such a stunning scene.

The order called for all tanks and wheeled vehicles to turn on their headlights and proceed to the specified defensive positions. To maintain uninterrupted movement of the wheeled vehicles through the mud, several tanks were designated as "tractors." They towed up to two wheeled vehicles each through some sections of road onto dry ground. If it was required, they returned for other wheeled vehicles and repeated the exercise.

By employing headlights, we were able to maintain normal speed given the road conditions. But the primary goal of the command was to demonstrate to the enemy that significant forces were being regrouped. An area many kilometers wide and deep was ablaze with light. It was like an avalanche of troops.

The fascist command cast about in search of a way to save their surrounded force. They brought up powerful forces from other sectors. If at the beginning there were three panzer and three infantry divisions operating against the outer encirclement ring, then by 11 February the enemy had brought in an additional five panzer and three infantry divisions.

Countless attacks launched by the Germans to break into the encircled forces were defeated. The forces of the First and Second Ukrainian *Fronts*, defending on the outer encirclement ring, were at the same time fighting to liquidate the enemy trapped in the pocket. The Soviet command delivered a surrender ultimatum to the encircled forces on 8 February, which the enemy rejected.

On 11 February, the command of Army Group South launched a decisive offensive against the outer encirclement ring. The 1st Panzer and 8th Army, with forces of up to eight panzer divisions, attacked from the areas west of Rizino and Erka toward Lysyanka. The encircled force attacked toward them, but this attempt to save the encircled formations and units also suffered defeat. By the morning of 17 February, the encircled forces had been liquidated. The enemy lost fifty-five thousand killed and more than eighteen thousand captured. Soviet troops captured an enormous amount of various types of combat equipment.

The Korsun-Shevchenkovskiy operation was one of the model operations for encirclement and destruction of a powerful enemy grouping. The inner and outer rings of encirclement were created simultaneously with the defeat of powerful enemy counterattacks and counterstrikes. Formations of the First and Second Ukrainian *Fronts* not only destroyed the powerful enemy grouping that had been caught in the ring but also defeated fifteen divisions, including eight panzer divisions, that were operating against the outer encirclement ring.

The employment of the tank armies—the 6th in the first echelon of the First Ukrainian *Front* for breaking through enemy defenses, and 5th Guards Tank Army and 6th Tank Army for defense on the outer encirclement ring—was an exception to the rule of Soviet military art.

The morning of 26 January 1944 was overcast. It was the second day of the tankers' offensive in unbelievably difficult weather conditions. It rained during the day, and wet clumps of snow fell at night. Visibility was poor in every direction. The enemy well understood that in these conditions, combat activities were possible only along roads. He took this into account in constructing his defense, concentrating his efforts on holding populated areas and the heights around them. At the same time, the terrain on the axis of the attack of the 5th Mechanized Corps abounded in numerous gullies and ravines—paths of concealed maneuver of the troops of both sides in dry weather. But in the muck, they were suitable only for the movement of small groups of infantry with small arms.

The enemy either held the areas between battle positions under observation or carried out periodic patrolling. Occasionally, he paid no attention to certain areas, considering them impassable. "One should take into consideration that which the enemy ignores!"

Units of the 156th Tank Regiment, 45th Mechanized Brigade, were proceeding along an improved dirt road that passed through Zhazhkov, Tynovka, and Lysyanka.[1] They were seven hundred to eight hundred meters short of Tynovka. The going was tough. The tanks of Lieutenant Gevorg Chobanyan were attacking straight ahead. The commander soon came to realize that a frontal attack against this enemy strongpoint would entail significant losses. Enemy antitank guns were firing. They had good fields of fire, particularly along the road. The enemy believed that the road was the only avenue of approach and had sited his weapons accordingly. The muzzle flash of a shot appeared from the area of a haystack. The track flew off one of the Shermans on the left flank of the combat formation. Chobanyan realized that its commander had not detected the origin of the enemy antitank round. Seconds mean everything in combat. The more so in a tank engagement. It would require priceless time to orient his subordinate in this situation. Traversing his turret ever so slightly, the company commander silenced the haystack with his main gun. A high-explosive round found its mark on the enemy gun and its crew.

Had the weather been good, and not slushy, the tankers could have easily negotiated this terrain. They had long ago developed a tactical drill: withdraw somewhat, then bypass the enemy resistance, and attack it on the flank or rear. It was standard procedure. But here the conditions were not so easy. Despite the difficulty, they accomplished the mission. And Chobanyan took a risk. It was completely justified. This aspect of the technical capability of the Sherman had somehow been forgotten. Under the pressure of events, however, he remembered. Just before the battle, during movement, the Emcha had demonstrated its traffic-ability in muddy terrain. This was a direct reflection of the ground pressure of the M4A2.[2]

Gevorg Avakovich decided to take advantage of the relative lightness of the Shermans and to defeat the enemy's fire in Tynovka with fewer losses. The weather had deteriorated even more, worsening the visibility toward the enemy. It was an opportune moment for carrying out Chobanyan's plan.

While the driver-mechanic and his assistant repaired the damaged tank, the gunner continued to fire the tank's weapons, drawing the defenders' attention to himself. Chobanyan left another tank near the road and led the remaining vehicles to the left, along the slope of a ravine. A ditchlike track lay on the surface of the softened chernozem, and the subsoil sustained the weight of the Emcha. Slowly but inexorably, the company crept around the north flank of Tynovka. Forty minutes had passed from the start of the flanking maneuver. The enemy had not detected the action of the bypassing group. The enemy failed to consider the foolhardiness of the Soviet tankers, who would risk crawling into a gully with rain-soaked soil. It turned out that this was not a fatal risk for the Shermans.

Gevorg Avakovich calculated that he had reached sufficient

depth in his bypass, and now he could attack. He gave a radio command to the two tanks on the road—on signal they were to move toward the enemy along the road. He would attack with the remainder of the company from the flank. The suddenness of the attack would double its effectiveness. It would stun the enemy and reduce the level of his resistance.

Having carried out a brief reconnaissance, the *desantniki*[3] determined that there were no defending enemy forces on the axis of the intended attack of the bypassing group. The enemy had not detected Chobanyan's company main body. He could delay no longer.

The signal was given. The attack commenced at reduced speed along the road. They were a small force, these two tanks, but they fired all their weapons. The other six Shermans attacked vigorously from the flank, with intensive main gun fires. The attack of Chobanyan's company fell like snow on the enemy's heads. Not more than two hundred meters remained to the village of Tynovka. The lieutenant ordered his subordinates to increase speed. The diesels revved, the cannons pumped out round after round. They had to reach the streets of this enemy strongpoint as quickly as possible. The intensity of the battle grew with each minute. The village's burning and destroyed homes were now becoming visible. Two muzzle flashes shone on the northwest outskirts of the town. A round slammed into the turret of a Sherman and, ricocheting, flew to the side. Despite the noise of the motors, driver-mechanic Senior Sergeant Markor'yants had turned his tank to face the threat. He quickly maneuvered the tank to the side and then drove forward.

The defenders realized what was happening and increased their fire against the flanking group. The submachine gunners had dismounted from several tanks and, moving through the mud, began to fall behind. Pity! They would be needed during the fight inside the village. Gevorg thoughtfully praised those soldiers who, despite the fire, remained on the tanks.

The Emcha of Aleksandr Sosnin, throwing up a mixture of mud and snow, careened through the gardens and yards. The lieutenant spotted a group of fascists with *panzerfausts* behind the ruins of a house. They were hurriedly occupying a firing position. This was Sosnin's first battle. A mound appeared several meters ahead, along his vehicle's path. Using abbreviated crew commands, the tank commander curtly ordered the driver, "Stop behind the mound!"

Its brakes squealing, the Sherman froze in place. The enemy antitank gunners, not realizing that they had been detected, were hurriedly preparing their weapons. Suddenly, they spotted our tank as it took up a covered position. They quickly ducked behind the house. But it was already too late. A precise burst of machine-gun fire forced them to the ground.

At the same time, a machine gun and several submachine guns rattled from the opposite side of the street. Our *tankodesantniki*, suppressed by the fire, also went to ground. A young infantry officer, his face blackened by gun smoke, ran toward Sosnin's tank. There was a brief conversation, normal in such situations. Without any delay, Aleksandr drove his tank toward the enemy targets to his front. The hurried forward rush of the Emcha stunned the enemy. The machine gunners and infantry attempted to save themselves by fleeing. But to no avail. Several were ground up under the tank's tracks. Throwing down their weapons, six Germans threw up their hands.

Combat in a built-up area is a series of rapidly flowing, fierce engagements with the enemy. Only continuous, mutually supporting fire and continuous forward pressure can achieve common success. The defenders were fighting stubbornly for the eastern portion of Tynovka, along the road to Pavlovka. Up to two squads of infantry, armed with *panzerfausts*, were supported by two antitank guns, with the possibility of tank positions in depth. Simply stated, this was a serious pocket of resistance that could not be taken from the march. It would be dangerous to attack head-on. There were too many antitank systems in the enemy position.

What to do now? The company commander pondered several alternatives. He could not maneuver—it was impossible inside the village. There was too much rubble of houses and outbuildings. It would not help to bypass the village on the left. There was a small grove of trees behind it, along the southern edge of the road, that would provide excellent concealment for antitank guns. These could fire effectively at the flanks of the attacking Shermans.

Only one option remained—to place the weight of the upcoming fight on the shoulders of the submachine gunners. They were fewer in number than before. But the *Emchisti* would support the attackers with heavy aimed fire. And while the *desantniki* bypassed nodes of enemy resistance, the tankers would attempt to decimate the enemy ranks with the power of their main gun fire. Mutual assistance. Chobanyan's tanks began to fire methodically at the enemy, who was seeking cover in the houses and vegetation. It prevented the enemy literally from raising up his head and firing precise bursts at our bypassing dismounts. Several precision volleys of the *Emchisti* destroyed both enemy guns and their ammunition carrier. They showered the more dangerous portions of the enemy position with high-explosive rounds and held these areas under continuous observation. The tankers were particularly zealous in searching out any suspected *panzerfaust* positions.

A green rocket arched into the sky—the signal that the submachine gunners had reached their attack position. Immediately a red rocket hissed upward—the command for the combined attack. The fierce twenty-minute battle began to die down. Displaying broken resistance, the enemy withdrew to the east. Darkness fell. Snow began to fall, then it began to storm. There could be no thought of pursuit. The company halted on a bare field 1.5 kilometers east of Tynovka. They were tired and hungry but satisfied with the just completed difficult fight.

The company commander decided to feed his tankers and *desantniki* with dry rations. He contacted the regimental commander to report the results of the fight for Tynovka and his present location. Chobanyan received information concerning the overall situation. The brigade main body, including the tank regiment, had beaten off an enemy counterattack from the south. The Germans had made ferocious attempts to liquidate the growing penetration into their defense. And so the tank company spent the night under the open sky. It was no joy to them that they were ordered to remain in position. Because of the poor weather, each platoon had to put out its own security. They had to remain alert in this weather, especially against enemy infiltrators.

The night passed quietly. The nervous company commander was at his post early in the morning. The sky was white, and snow continued to fall. The Shermans were white hillocks. At times, gusts of wind blew aside the shroud of precipitation. Chobanyan

15 *Rain, Snow, and Mud*

looked around at the southern slope of the hill on which his company stood. He blinked his eyes in disbelief. Below him some four hundred meters, blanketed in the same snow covering, stood seven or eight German Tiger tanks. The enemy was sleeping quietly, within submachine-gun range of each other. The darkness and storm had brought the sides, as they say, shoulder to shoulder. And then they had gone to ground. What now? The lieutenant feverishly sought a solution. In such a critical situation, he who opened fire first would have the upper hand.

Gevorg Avakovich climbed up to awake the crew of the closest Emcha, warning them to maintain noise discipline. He summoned his platoon commanders. Quickly explaining the situation to them, he showed them the enemy tanks that could be discerned on the terrain. Not a single person was visible. The bad weather had driven the Germans inside their vehicles.

Chobanyan's company began hurried preparation to commence firing. As a precaution, with the beginning of the heavy snowfall the night before, all gunners had stuffed rags in the turret apertures for their telescopic sights and coaxial machine guns. They had closed the covers over the commanders' periscopes. It was a simple matter to remove these elemental protections of the tanks' optical instruments, and in just a few moments, the guns were prepared for firing. The main guns were loaded and traversed to the proper deflection. The company commander waited minute by minute for daybreak to bring light to the morning sky. Everyone awaited the command: Fire! That they would destroy the enemy was a certainty. But the anticipated command did not come. Anxious moments passed. It seemed that their nerves were tingling. Gevorg's eyes teared up from the pressure. He got hold of himself. Be calm! Patience! Nothing had been lost yet. They simply had to wait for visibility to improve. No one could make it happen. Mother Nature had her own laws, not subject to man.

Somewhere in the heavens, above the low clouds, the sun rose, invisible from the ground. The weather slowly began to improve. The snow precipitation fell off with each minute, and soon it ceased altogether. Would they wait much longer? How slowly time passed. This was always the case when one awaited something or someone important. The air began to clear. The targets were not sharp, but they were visible just the same. It was time for a salvo. Fire!

Four simultaneous shots tore through the early morning silence. Two Tigers went up in flames. On the remainder, the turret hatches began to clank open. The enemy tankers, awakened in ignorance from their sleep, twisted their heads around searching for the firing enemy tanks. The second Sherman salvo gave them their final wake-up call. Three more Tigers were set afire. There were no answering shots. Some time later, it was established that there could be none. All the gunsight apertures in the turrets were packed full of snow.

Taking advantage of the smoke screen from burning Tigers, undamaged vehicles were hurrying in the direction of Pavlovka. The *Emchisti* celebrated. In such an unbelievable situation that had arisen out of pure chance, they had found themselves the victor.

An hour passed after this little disagreement with their neighbor. The sounds of the motors of heavy German armored vehicles reached the ears of our tankers. The sounds grew louder. There was no doubt. The enemy was moving in more forces for a counterattack, in all probability Tigers or Panthers. And doubtless accompanied by infantry.

Chobanyan again had to rack his brain in considering many unknowns: How much force was the enemy bringing forward? What was their mission? Would the remaining units of the 156th Regiment arrive soon? There were no answers to all these questions.

Gevorg Avakovich decided once again to rely upon the earlier tested principle—the reduced ground pressure of the tanks. For us *inomarochniki*, it would be a true and faithful servant over the course of the entire two months of traveling along the broken-down, muddy Ukrainian roads and occasional plowed field.

One of the peculiarities of the front-line period was that the more complex the situation became, the more sharply one's mind operated. The commander had to think only about himself and the mission, not about the actions of his subordinates. He had quickly to find an effective means of anticipating the enemy's actions, then to defeat him, and all of this with minimal losses to his own force.

Chobanyan instantly conceived a plan—to avoid a head-on clash with the enemy, he would evade for some period of time and be careful. Using the trafficability of the Shermans across the soggy ground, he would concentrate them along ravines and gullies. The heavy enemy tanks would not risk traversing these areas. And he would employ the submachine gunners for close-in security and at the same time send them out on reconnaissance.

The plan was implemented. The Emchas quickly dropped down off the hill and in pairs dispersed north of Tynovka in a long gully, where there were also some spurs and smaller ditches.

Six Tigers and up to two platoons of infantry in two armored transporters, with some of them sitting atop their vehicles, approached Tynovka. The German vehicles halted about six hundred meters short of the village, refusing to risk entry into the village. It appeared that they feared the presence of antitank guns. The *desantniki* warily observed them, prepared at any moment to block the path of the enemy infantry by fire should they dismount for a counterattack or to inspect the terrain. In the event that battle was engaged, three Shermans maneuvering from behind the hill would support the *desantniki* with main gun and machine-gun fire.

The enemy Tigers and infantry did not have the stomach for combat. The heavy beasts turned their long barrels on Tynovka and its northern approaches and fired two high-explosive rounds. It was more as a warning. Then they unhurriedly crawled off down the road toward the east. The damp chernozem cornfields were not for them. They would become bogged down in an instant. It was a known fact that their ground pressure was 1.5 times greater than that of the Emcha. They would have been unable to maneuver.

"Hunting with Borzois"

I do not know who first used hunting terms to describe the means developed by *Emchisti* for combating heavy German tanks. It was not for a lark that we had to resort to this tactic in the Korsun-Shevchenkovskiy operation (January–February 1944).

The tanks of the two sides were far from equal in firepower. The Tiger and Panther were equipped with a long-barreled 88-mm

cannon. The Shermans also had a long gun, but of lesser caliber—
76.2 mm. The 85- to 100-mm frontal and turret armor of the
enemy tanks made them practically invulnerable to the Emcha's
projectiles at those points. But they did burn and could be immobilized in place by our precision shooting.

The Korsun-Shevchenkovskiy operation of two Ukrainian
Fronts began on 26 January 1944. The recently created 6th Tank
Army, to which the 5th Mechanized Corps belonged, was attacking in the southeastward direction toward Zvenigorodka from
the area north of Tynovka. The 5th Guards Tank Army of the
adjacent First Ukrainian *Front* was attacking from the opposite
direction to converge with it. In coordination with infantry formations, these tank armies were to encircle significant enemy
forces in the Korsun-Shevchenkovskiy bulge.

Beginning on the morning of 27 January, the 233d Tank Brigade—the backbone of the corps' forward detachment—received
the mission not to become engaged in protracted battles for isolated enemy strongpoints but to penetrate into Zvenigorodka,
where it was to close the ring of encirclement.

At midday, the brigade's 1st Tank Battalion, with *tankodesantniki* aboard, reached the outskirts of a large and important, in the
operational-tactical sense, inhabited area—Lysyanka [135 kilometers south of Kiev]. The enemy, realizing the key significance
of this strongpoint, had concentrated up to a battalion of infantry,
reinforced by five Tiger tanks, to hold it.

Lysyanka—a small regional town—stretched out in a deep hol-
low. Its houses could be seen only from a close vantage point. The
Germans had dug in on the heights that framed this inhabited
locale. They were covering the road and heights adjoining it with
dense interlocking fires from all weapons. The defenders paid
almost no attention to the gullies and ravines. They believed that
their bottoms and side slopes, deteriorated from the bad weather,
were unsuitable for deploying tanks.

We had to seize Lysyanka as rapidly as possible. The most
important targets in its defenses were the tanks. They had to be
knocked out in the first assault. It would then be much easier
to deal with the infantry. The accomplishment of this task was
further complicated by the worsening weather—the rain was
growing heavier.

Captain Nikolay Maslyukov, the battalion commander, made

the following decision: two tank platoons were to attack the enemy along the highway (demonstration group), and the platoon of Junior Lieutenant Mikhail Prikhod'ko, moving along the side of one of the broad gullies, was to reach the flank of the Tigers and attack them with armor-piercing rounds on their hulls. This concept followed the model of "hunting with Borzois": the dogs tantalize the wolf from the front, while several hounds come at him from the flanks to take him down.

Our tanks maintained radio silence to achieve surprise in this unusual attack. Only the radios of the battalion commander and the two platoons attacking along the road were left on. Nikolay Maslyukov quietly orchestrated the actions of the demonstration and flanking groups. The successful accomplishment of the battalion's mission depended on their skillful efforts.

Attentively studying the surrounding terrain, Prikhod'ko noticed nothing except dripping wet shrubbery and the occasional modest tree. The Emchas of his platoon crept forward on idling motors, avoiding movement along the same track. There was the possibility of getting bogged down in the soggy chernozem. As before, visibility was poor. A head wind hurled large raindrops into their faces and carried the noise of their laboring engines from their sterns into the endless steppe. This encouraged the tankers because it provided additional security for their actions. It would have been worse for the wind to be blowing toward the enemy. "Today, the weather is our friend," the platoon commander said encouragingly to his crew.

Hundreds of meters of a difficult path lay behind. Prikhod'ko understood that his tanks could encounter the enemy at any moment, and he was not wrong. Up ahead, Mikhail noticed a mound—a small ground sheet hung suspended above the ground. It was motionless. Out from under the tarpaulin crawled a German soldier, who stared at the lead tank, clearly not knowing if it was his or ours. Without hesitation, the driver-mechanic veered his Sherman toward the enemy position and ground the soldier and his covered machine gun into the earth. The enemy's security outpost had been destroyed without a sound. This did not happen often. "The defender's main forces are somewhere nearby," the platoon commander concluded to himself. A sheet of heavy rain hid the horizon from view. The enemy position was somewhere up ahead—but it could not be discerned.

Prikhod'ko reported his engagement with the enemy outpost to the battalion commander and received the order to stop. The demonstration group along the road began its spirited "teasing" attack, trying to attract the defenders' attention completely to itself. By doing this, it simplified for Prikhod'ko's crews the accomplishment of their mission.

The Shermans of the flanking group froze in place, their motors quietly idling. The commands of the officers of the tanks attacking frontally sounded crisply in the headphones. Frequent machine-gun bursts and the noise of motors were reported. The main part of the concept of "hunting with Borzois" had been accomplished successfully.

At this time, somewhere in the heights a strong gust of wind dispersed the heavy curtain of clouds, and a broad patch of sky shone through. The rain halted. Would it hold off long? A moment! A fortuitous moment! Prikhod'ko fixed his glance at the unfolding view. Some seventy meters ahead loomed two immense black-crossed tanks. Their main guns patrolled the road, prepared at any moment to greet our tanks attacking from the front with deadly fire.

Two Shermans of Prikhod'ko's platoon, moving in echelon, had stopped at the same time. This enabled them to open fire quickly, without interfering with each other. Their main guns had long ago been loaded with armor-piercing rounds. "The right Tiger is yours, the left one is mine. Fire!" commanded Mikhail.

Main gun fires ripped through the damp, cold air. The engine compartment of the right beast was enveloped in flames. The left Tiger shook from the strike of the solid shot but did not catch fire. Prikhod'ko shouted to the gunner, "Finish him off!" The second armor-piercing round did its work—the clumsy target belched black smoke. The German tankers began to jump out of their vehicle. Accurate machine-gun fires found their mark.

The Emchas attacked forcefully along the road, conducting intensive main gun and machine-gun fires. Prikhod'ko's platoon also did not spare their ammunition. Having been attacked from two sides, the enemy began to withdraw under fire to the south. Minutes later, the lead tanks of Maslyukov's battalion, in coordination with their *desantniki,* burst upon the enemy positions. Lysyanka stretched out below.

The *Emchisti* participating in the defeat of enemy attempts to break out of the Korsun-Shevchenkovskiy ring employed a different method of combat with the enemy's heavy tanks. Two Shermans were designated in each platoon for each single attacking Tiger. One tank fired armor-piercing shells at one or the other track, the other tank awaited the moment when the undamaged track had driven the German tank into a 90-degree turn, exposing its entire flank. Then it delivered a solid shot into the fuel cell. As a rule, attacking enemy tanks were permitted to close to four hundred to five hundred meters. It was difficult to break a track at greater ranges.

A "Psychological" Attack

Each officer at the front had his own moment in the sun, a specific day (or days) and a defined place. For Captain Nikolay Maslyukov, this was Lysyanka. This, indeed, was the peak of his command talent. Without a doubt, new aspects of the gifted battalion commander clearly would shine forth in other battles. But the time of his death was near. Maslyukov perished at 1300 on 28 January 1944 in Zvenigorodka. We were doggedly fighting our way there.

The wildly fluctuating weather continued. The brief pause was sufficient only for the capture of the important heights on the approaches to Lysyanka. Even more heavy rain fell later and, with the coming of dawn, abundant wet snow. Like it or not, this enemy strongpoint had to be taken at night.

Nikolay Maslyukov assembled the company and tank commanders and explained the developing situation. At this time the crews replenished their Emchas' ammunition supply. A stubborn fight in a built-up area lay ahead, at night. Nikolay Nikolayevich listened to the opinions of his company commanders and several platoon commanders. All arrived at the same conclusion: attack Lysyanka without delay, bringing all the firepower of their Shermans to bear on the enemy, and, as before, not sparing main gun rounds or machine-gun bullets.

The captain agreed with his subordinates' opinion. He himself added: "We will augment the strength of our fire attack by turning on our lights and blowing our sirens at full power. We will conduct a 'psychological' attack!"

The Emchas had modest headlights, with a sufficiently powerful beam. And a wailing signaling device—a siren. When it was turned on, even the tankers, who knew its voice, experienced tingling in their spines. How would it affect someone who was hearing it for the first time? And at full power? Could he keep his nerve?

All was prepared for the tanks' rush into the northwest outskirts of Lysyanka. Then came Captain Maslyukov's terse command: "Turn on lights and sirens! Forward!"

Though years have passed, the picture of this unusual attack is clear in my mind in all its detail. The piercing light of the headlamps pulled the road out of the darkness, along with the adjacent fields, houses, and trees. It blinded the enemy infantry and artillery gun crew. The powerful howl of the sirens ripped into the night. It assaulted the eardrums and placed a heavy load on the brain. The enemy fire, initially somewhat dense, began to weaken. The "psychological" attack bore fruit. "Any means is good in battle: blind the enemy, destroy him with the tank!"

From the first moment of the attack, the Sherman crews conducted intense main gun and machine-gun fires. When the enemy's resistance had noticeably weakened, Maslyukov sternly ordered: "Conserve ammunition! Use your tracks!"

Each platoon and tank commander, emerging partially from his hatch, could easily see the enemy in the illuminated surroundings. Using their intercom systems, they gave commands to the driver-mechanic, directing their Emchas toward observed targets. Assault troops carrying submachine guns ran nearby, shielding "their" Sherman from *panzerfaust* gunners. The armor plate of antitank guns cracked. The multiton mass of the "American" easily overran the defenders' mortars and machine guns. The soft, wet earth received the debris into its cold embrace without resistance.

Maslyukov's battalion and the submachine gunners of the brigade commander's reserve captured Lysyanka without losses. Some twenty kilometers remained to the city of Zvenigorodka.

Friendly Fire

After the conclusion of the Korsun-Shevchenkovskiy operation, the forces of the Second Ukrainian *Front*, commanded by Marshal of the Soviet Union I. S. Konev, were opposed by the 8th Army of Army Group South. The decision was made to conduct the Umansk-Botoshansk operation (5 March–17 April 1944), to liberate the southwestern oblasts of Ukraine. This operation was part of the strategic offensive of Soviet forces in the right-bank Ukraine in 1943–44.

The *front* commander's concept envisaged the defeat of the 8th Army, the breaking up of Army Group South, and the blocking of the path of retreat of the 1st Panzer Army in the southern axis, cooperating with the First Ukrainian *Front* for its defeat. The main blow was struck from the line Vinograd-Zvenigorodka-Shpola toward Uman by forces of the 27th, 52d, and 4th Guards Armies, 2d, 5th, and 6th Tank Armies (415 tanks and 147 self-propelled guns altogether), the 5th Guards Cavalry Corps, and also a portion of the forces of the 40th and 53d Armies. The 7th and 5th Guards Armies launched a supporting attack from the area of Kirovograd in the direction of Novoukrainka. These ground actions were supported by the 5th Air Army.

The offensive was begun on 5 March and developed successfully. On the first day, the 2d and 5th Guards Tank Armies were introduced into the fight to strengthen the attack on the main axis. On the third day of the operation, they forced the Gornyy Tikich River from the march, broke through the last defensive line occupied by the enemy on the path to the Southern Bug River, and began pursuing him. The 6th Tank Army was moving right behind them. Having captured Uman on 10 March, the forward detachments of the armies reached the Southern Bug. The 6th Tank Army was committed to support the high tempo of the offensive. Crossing the Southern Bug River, the tank armies surged toward the Dniester.

Conditions for the actions of the troops were exceptionally

difficult. The rivers were running full and the roads and fields were a sea of mud. Only tracked vehicles could move, and the wheeled vehicles remained in assembly areas. In units of the 5th Mechanized Corps, Sherman tanks were used almost like draft animals. Fuel cells were mounted on their armor, along with boxes of shells and ammunition, and *desantniki.*

During his retreat in the areas of Uman and Khristinovka, the enemy had abandoned an enormous quantity of combat equipment and vehicles. We siphoned diesel fuel from these vehicles and topped off our tanks, conserving our own supplies.

Combat units were confined, for the most part, to the roads. Beyond the Dniester River, Sherman tanks began to experience a shortage of main gun rounds. Aviation came to our assistance, dropping ammunition by parachute.

On 17 March, forward units of the right wing of the Second Ukrainian *Front* captured a bridgehead on the right bank of the Dniester in an area south of the city of Mogilev-Podol'skiy. Favorable conditions had been created for the subsequent offensive into the depth of the enemy's defenses.

Pursuing the enemy, the 27th and 52d Armies along with formations of the 2d and 6th Tank Armies arrived at the Soviet-Romanian border along an eighty-five-kilometer front on 26 March. On the night of 28 March, forces of the Second Ukrainian *Front* forced the Prut River from the march and initiated combat operations on the territory of Romania.

As a result of the Umansk-Botoshansk operation, the 8th Army and a portion of the 1st Panzer Army were defeated, and the front of Army Group South was broken. Ten enemy divisions had lost 50 to 75 percent of their personnel and almost all their heavy armaments. In the course of the operation, forces of the *front* had advanced some 200 to 250 kilometers, liberated a significant portion of the right-bank Ukraine and Modavia, and reached the northeast region of Romania.

Spring 1944. The Umansk-Botoshansk offensive operation was conducted in the most difficult conditions of the spring thaw. The thickness of the sticky layer of chernozem reached almost forty to fifty centimeters [fifteen to eighteen inches] on all the roads.

After a nineteen-day offensive, units of the 5th Mechanized Corps seized the important crossroads at Vapnyarka [250 kilometers southwest of Kiev] on 15 March. This opened the way for a strong push to the south, toward the Dniester River. Only tanks could take full advantage of this opportunity. An assault group of four to five submachine gunners headed by a sergeant, and sometimes an officer, was placed on the Shermans and self-propelled guns in all the corps' brigades. Each combat vehicle also carried two or three crates of ammunition and one or two diesel fuel drums. This not insignificant load sharply reduced the maneuverability of the tanks and self-propelled guns. In the weather situation that had developed, there was no alternative. The wheeled supply columns would remain in the Vapnyarka area until the roads dried out.

Seventeen Shermans of the 45th Mechanized Brigade, commanded by Major Troshin, received the order to march quietly to the city of Mogilev-Podol'skiy [on the Dniester River, three hundred kilometers southwest of Kiev] and cut the enemy's path of retreat across the Dniester River.

The tanks of Lieutenant Evgeniy Shapkin and Junior Lieutenant Yuriy Orekhov, acting as flank guard, were approaching the town through a long ravine with gently sloping sides. It was unbelievably difficult to move in the plowed-up sticky mud. Shapkin's tank became stuck at one of the gully's twists. The *tankodesantniki* immediately dismounted and fanned out to set up covering positions for the tank on both sides of the ravine.

Orekhov's tank approached Shapkin's stuck Sherman, and the assistant driver-mechanic quickly hooked his tow cables onto the mired tank. Yuriy, standing in front of his Emcha, began to give the hand signals to the driver-mechanic. The recovery was under way. Suddenly, the submachine gunners on the left crest of the ravine cried out: "Germans!" At the same time, they commenced automatic weapons fire, withdrawing toward their tanks.

The crews quickly occupied their combat stations. They managed to cram the hurrying *desantniki* into their turrets also. Soon the Germans (not less than 150 soldiers and officers) approached close enough to the "connected" tanks to throw grenades. It was already too late to return fire. Seconds later, the Germans were on top of the Shermans like glaze. They covered the vision blocks with mud and smeared chernozem on the telescope openings in the turret, totally blinding the crew. Pounding on the hatches, they tried to open them with rifle bayonets. All the while, they were shouting: "Rus, kaput! Give up!"

The right flank security group, coming under fire, began to withdraw toward the highway. Two soldiers died and three were wounded in the lopsided encounter with the enemy. With enormous difficulty, they managed to reach the road. Fortunately, here they spotted two approaching Katyusha trucks.[1] Their commander, Guards Junior Lieutenant Ivan Krivtsov, listening to the submachine gunners' worried account, did not interrupt them. He made a murderous decision: to launch a direct-fire salvo at the German troops swarming the tanks. There was nothing else he could do. The enemy had overwhelming superiority. Any delay would surely result in the death of the tankers. The range to the target was minimal. The launch vehicles quickly planted their front wheels in the ditch. In this position they could quickly fire on the captured Shermans.[2] Several crucial minutes passed from the moment of the Katyushas' arrival until they fired their salvo. Brilliant trails of fire streaked toward the ravine with shrieks and hissing. In an instant, blinding flames danced up around the Emchas. The heartrending cries of the enemy infantry echoed in the gully. Did our own men survive the firestorm?

The smoke gradually drifted away. At first glance, the tanks stood undamaged. Their hulls and turrets were covered with thick soot. The hapless Germans were running in various directions. But they did not run far. The tankers opened fire on the fleeing enemy with a storm of machine-gun fire. At this time, the 233d Tank Brigade matériel support units arrived. Guards Junior Lieutenant Krivtsov loudly commanded: "Kill the Fritzes!"[3]

With shouts of "Ura-a-a!" support soldiers rushed into the attack. Several minutes later, the engagement subsided. Forty still-dazed prisoners glanced timidly in all directions. The remnants of the enemy units defeated east of the Dniester did not manage to break through to the west bank of this water obstacle.

Emchisti began to appear at open hatches. Our soldiers hurried over to them. "How do you feel, comrades, after such a fire 'baptism'?" they asked. Shapkin spread his hands, then pointed at his ears and, after a moment of silence, said, "One hundred bells are ringing in my head. I do not recommend such a working over to any of you. Even if you are protected by the armor of a tank."

Ivan Krivtsov walked over. He apologized for the fire strike on our own troops. "In this most dangerous situation that had developed, I had no other choice." Evgeniy Shapkin embraced and exchanged kisses with the artillery officer. "Thank you, friend, for the help! Not so much because your effort was so extraordinary, but because you had the courage to do it. Anything can happen in war. Sometimes the situation forces one to fire on one's own troops in order to defeat the enemy!"

Everyone was smiling.

Having repaired the damaged track and pulled down their charred tarpaulins, the *Emchisti* departed for Mogilev-Podol'skiy.

The Darkness and Wind Are Our Friends

The city of Bel'tsy [105 kilometers northwest of Kishinev in Moldova] was just a stone's throw away. Major Fedor Sazonov, commander of the 233d Tank Brigade, directed the units that were surging ahead hurriedly to reach the eastern quarter of this important operational objective. In day-to-day activities, and the more so on the battlefield, "an order will not always be detailed."

During the afternoon of 23 March 1944, our attack was held up almost four kilometers from Bel'tsy. A small hill some eight hundred meters to the left of the road turned out to be a particularly strong nut to crack. By holding this hill, the enemy covered the approaches to the city. Several antitank guns and a mortar battery in this strongpoint had the road in their sights. Artillery deployed in positions somewhere behind the hill added their dense fire, as well.

The hill could not be bypassed on the right. A plowed field, soaked by the rains, stretched to the horizon. There remained only to await nightfall and then attack this key enemy point of resistance under cover of darkness. We needed infantry, the more the better. The brigade had only one and one-half companies of *tankodesantniki*. We had to be satisfied with that small number.

The companies of Senior Lieutenant Ivan Yakushkin and Senior Lieutenant Aleksandr Kuchma from the 1st Battalion were designated to support the infantry in this attack. The tankers topped off their supply of high-explosive main gun rounds, receiving many from other brigade units. There was no time to consider bringing up a resupply of ammunition from the rear. Our aviation delivered a fresh supply by parachute a day later.

The brigade commander made the following decision. With the onset of dusk, move the tanks quietly (using only one motor) to the start positions in a dried riverbed, some two hundred meters from the forward edge of the enemy defenses. From this position, upon a common signal, the force was to rain fire from all tank weapons on the hill, and then the *desantniki*, supported by the companies of Yakushkin and Kuchma, were to attack and capture the objective.

Having listened to the brigade commander's plan, Ivan Yakushkin requested permission for his company to deviate from it slightly. The essence of his request was as follows: one platoon would remain to attack from the front along with the tanks of Aleksandr Kuchma. He—Yakushkin—using one motor at low revolutions per minute, would lead the remaining two platoons along a gully reconnoitered during daylight into the rear of the enemy position. He would have ten *desantniki* riding on his tanks for reconnaissance and security. A strong, gusty wind, blowing away from the enemy, would substantially aid in accomplishing the planned flanking maneuver. This was "small change," which we would not once consider in subsequent battles. But in this case, Kuchma's tanks and the remaining platoon of Ivan Ignat'ev's company had to make as many sorties as possible to the forward edge. They had to attract the maximum possible attention of the defending enemy to themselves. Upon a green star cluster signal, indicating that the flanking tanks had reached their assault line in the enemy's rear, a simultaneous attack would be launched from the front and rear.

The brigade commander attentively listened to Yakushkin's suggestion. He asked several pointed questions: "Is the gully sufficiently large to support your concealed maneuver? In the event the flanking group is detected, what will it do?"

Ivan Yakushkin reported the following to Major Sazonov: the northern slopes of the gully along which the tanks would maneuver offered good trafficability. Not more than two Emchas would move along the same track. Upon the enemy's detection of our maneuver, he would immediately fire a green rocket and quickly begin the attack—our group from the flank or rear, depending on the depth of its penetration into the enemy's zone—and the main forces under the command of Kuchma from the front.

The brigade commander was not offended, although at first glance he had reason to be. His plan had been substantially altered. "The matter at hand is more important than the ego" was a golden rule of our bitter war experiences. A sensible thought at the front line is very often respected. The more so that in this case because it came from an experienced officer, Ivan Yaku-shkin, who had been in the active army since the first day of the Great Patriotic War. Sazonov had himself been fighting Germans for about two years.

The brigade commander approved the plan of action suggested by Yakushkin and immediately gave the necessary instructions.

The crews set about in preparation for the night attack. In Yakushkin's company, they carefully inspected the tie-downs on the hulls of their Emchas: pioneer tools,[1] tow cables (nothing should be a source of giveaway noise). In combat, serious losses could result from overlooked details. By evening, the wind had increased in velocity; at times, rain drizzled down. The tankers were happy with such weather, the worse the better!

Darkness covered the earth, steaming from the day's warmth. It was time to move. Kuchma's subordinates, Yakushkin's attached platoon, and the *desantniki* began carefully to move forward to their start position for the frontal attack on the hill. Fifteen minutes later, Yakushkin's flanking group departed. It withdrew one kilometer into their own rear, then turned to the northwest and quickly took up their selected movement route. The Shermans quietly idled along on one motor (375 horsepower), the rubber-cushioned tracks laying down almost noiselessly in the soft chernozem. Four submachine gunners went 150 to 200 meters ahead, acting in the role of a reconnaissance patrol. The tank commanders, having dismounted, led their Shermans along, trying to avoid having more than two tanks follow the same track.

Three kilometers of dirt path lay behind them. Ivan Ignat'evich sat on the turret of the lead tank. Straining his eyes, he stared into the darkness. He would not miss the signal from the patrol indicating detection of the enemy. The wind drove large raindrops into his face. Yakushkin thoughtfully welcomed its timely discomfort.

All the crews spotted two blue flashes of a pocket flashlight ("the enemy is nearby"). They immediately cut their motors, as had been agreed to earlier. Waiting a little bit ahead of Yakushkin, Sergeant Aleksandr Pronin, the commander of the reconnaissance patrol, appeared out of the darkness. He reported his findings: the *desantniki* had reached several enemy dugouts. They had heard German speech. They were continuing to listen and observe.

Having gathered his officers, Ivan Yakushkin declared: "This completes the silent portion of our move. Whether there are many or few enemy, we will attack! A sudden strike is the guarantor of success! The enemy does not expect us. Too bad for him! Do not fire—use your tracks!"

Several minutes later, all was in readiness for the final rush. The company commander only regretted that he had not managed to bypass the hill a bit deeper. He had to attack the enemy position not from the rear, as he had intended, but from the flank.

The *desantniki* acting as scouts returned to their tanks. Yakushkin mounted them on the armor of his own Emcha. According to analysis of the data collected on the positions they had observed, there were up to two infantry squads reinforced by machine guns. This probably was the combat outpost.

The Shermans' motors worked harmoniously at full power. At the exact same second, an illumination rocket, hissing angrily, arched into the sky. After the battle, Ivan Ignat'evich said, "One could only dream of such a gift from the enemy!" In their fear, the Fritzes lit up themselves and us. The trajectory of the rocket they fired was almost vertical.

From this moment began the headlong energetic actions of the flanking group. Yakushkin reported his discovery of the enemy and the commencement of his attack to the brigade commander.

Seven tanks executed a right turn almost simultaneously and surged forward in a combat line into the enemy positions. Reinforcing materials cracked and splintered, and enemy infantry thrown into disarray cried out. Not dismounting, our *tanko-desantniki* sprayed them with submachine-gun bursts. Several illumination rockets were fired from the hill's crest toward Yakushkin's group. Mortars fired, but their shells landed and exploded far behind the attacking Shermans. It is not so simple to conduct mortar fire in night conditions. Every second, the sky was lit up with the light shafts of the "candles." Beyond the hill blinked the muzzle flashes of an artillery salvo, and three flares hung over the company's formation.

Ivan Yakushkin ordered his tank commander, Junior Lieutenant Ivan Filin, to fire a green rocket. Two kilometers to the right, the main guns of Aleksandr Kuchma's company immediately opened fire. The frontal attack against the hill had begun.

A second volley of enemy mortar rounds fired at the flanking tanks was more accurate. Three *desantniki* were wounded. Yakushkin's group could not hold their guns silent any longer. "Fire! Fire!" the company commander ordered. The geysers of bursting high-explosive shells fired from the east and south covered the slopes of the hill. The infantry and tanks were conducting a simultaneous assault on the Germans' defenses from two sides. The enemy's predicament was unpleasant, to say the least.

The pulse of a night fight can be easily sensed according to the strength of the fires of the opposing sides along particular sectors of the engagement line. It was now sufficiently high on the axis of Kuchma's attacking company. It was weaker against Yakushkin's company. But the enemy artillery continued to illuminate their combat formation and covered the left flank of the Shermans attacking from the south with two artillery strikes. The suspension was damaged on two tanks in Junior Lieutenant Konstantin Stepanov's platoon. Yakushkin ordered these immobile tanks to fire into the German artillery positions, to force the enemy to weaken, if not cease, his firing against the flanking group.

The remaining tanks of Yakushkin's group, conducting intensive main gun fire on the move, continued their attack. Their engines roared intensely as the Emchas moved along the unplowed soil. Behind them remained the deep trails of tracks. The *desantniki*, having dismounted, gathered into groups in the wake of the tanks, where they were covered from enemy rifle and machine-gun fires. Kuchma reported by radio to the brigade commander that his unit had seized the eastern slopes of the hill. The enemy was holding onto the crest with a small force. Yakushkin rejoiced at these words. He ordered his tank to halt. With three main gun salvos from the Emchas' position, the defense of the southwestern slopes of the hill collapsed. The smoke of the explosions had not yet dissipated when the Shermans lurched forward and ground all that remained in the Germans' positions under their tracks.

Not stopping, the tanks turned to the left and hurried toward the enemy artillery positions. Ivan Ignat'evich ordered Stepanov's crews to cease firing into the area he had earlier designated to prevent the attacking tanks from coming under their own fire.

The eastern sky showed red. Quiet descended on the hill. The enemy had lost about one hundred soldiers and officers, and twenty were captured; eight mortars, three antitank guns, five light and two heavy machine guns were destroyed; and four 75-mm field guns were crushed. Our losses were three Shermans destroyed. We could hardly have achieved these results with a daylight attack. "Night is our sister, ready to conceal and help us!"

The road to Bel'tsy was open!

The effectiveness of the method "attack the enemy from two sides and inflict rapidly discernible losses on him!" once again received a good practical confirmation. Company commanders Kuchma and Yakushkin were decorated with Orders of the Red Banner by order of the tank army commander, General A. G. Kravchenko.

The Emcha Plows

By 28 March 1944, the tanks of the 5th Mechanized Corps, with assault troops on board, had fought their way across nearly three hundred kilometers of territory and had reached the Prut River in the sector of Skulen' and Ungeny [twenty kilometers east of Jassy, Romania]. The Umansk-Botoshansk offensive operation concluded on this axis.

An order arrived in the 1st Battalion from the headquarters of the 233d Tank Brigade: send an officer on a tank back along the route of march of our offensive. His mission was to collect all repaired combat vehicles (twelve vehicles had been left behind) and direct them to Skulen'. The dispatch of such a guide was necessary because the end point of our brigade's actions had changed during the course of the offensive. Matériel support units delayed by muddy roads and crews of broken-down or damaged Shermans did not know of the change. They had to be reoriented.

Captain Aleksandr Kogan, the battalion commander, ordered me to carry out this unusual mission. Our preparations were hasty. We took aboard two containers of diesel fuel and several days' dry rations. Then we departed.

Our journey lasted two weeks. We marveled at what we saw in a land where fierce battles had just concluded: burned-out homes and entire forests reduced to ashes. It was time for planting spring wheat. But where would the seed come from? The Germans had carried everything out with them. Kitchen gardens were overrun with tall weeds. What could be used to plow them? The collective farms had neither horses nor tractors. A cow, if it had survived, could be used to pull a plow. But this was an extreme measure for a peasant. In such a case, they always said, "Harness the family's wet nurse to the plow. Have you lost your mind, friend!"

Three years of German occupation. The peasantry had even begun to forget how a cow moos. Single women and weak old men remained in the villages. All the concerns of life were on their shoulders: feeding the children, plowing the land, gathering the harvest. These were the consequences of the Germans' "new order."

Having carried out our mission, I was returning to the brigade's area with two Shermans. The sun was setting in the west. In front of us was the village of Chernovtsy. I decided to lager here for the night and hit the road again early in the morning, but the circumstances introduced a substantial adjustment to my plan. They forced us to forget about rest.

Upon approaching the first huts in Chernovtsy, the tankers were stunned by what they saw: five women, some with a frayed rope thrown over their shoulders, one holding old reins, struggling to drag a single-bladed plow. A sixth woman steered the plow, walking along the furrow. I got mad enough to boil water. I understood. These peasants were not doing this for the pleasure of it. Their predicament forced them to become "boatmen" on their own land (we knew about the Volga boatmen from our history).

I commanded the column to halt and jumped down onto the road from the lead tank. I walked quickly over to the "plowmen." A plan for subsequent actions formed immediately in my mind. The women, their faces streaked with sweat, stopped and began to look in my direction. They responded to my greeting with a traditional Ukrainian reply, "Be healthy!"

Barely catching my breath, I blurted out, "Don't wear yourself out! We will cultivate all your gardens! Where is the *kolkhoz* [collective farm] representative?" A young peasant wife, one of the "shaft horses," responded, "Old women, rest for a moment. I will come right back." She led me to a hut on the opposite side of the road. "Hanna Ivanovna is in charge of our *kolkhoz*. She is at home, sick." I called the tank commanders over and explained my unusual decision to them.

We would plow the gardens with the Shermans.

Hanna Ivanovna received our suggestion with enormous relief and joy. The main problem was to find a plow. It turned out that there were only two suitable for the task. "I have to ask around. I think I can find several," said the *kolkhoz* representative. "You cannot imagine the tremendous help you are giving to our village, with so many womenfolk here. We have no men—the Germans drove some off, and some went to the front."

We had another, not less important, concern. How would we harness the plows to the tanks? The *kolkhoz* representative looked over at my guide. "Oksana knows a little bit about blacksmithing." "My father taught me a little bit," the farrier's daughter bashfully related. "Unfortunately, the forge has not been fired up in a long time."

Hanna Ivanovna turned to me with a request. "Please, help start the fire in the forge. Oksana will show you how to do it. She has the skilled hands of a man," the *kolkhoz* representative proudly concluded.

Our conversation lasted almost an hour. The news about the help promised by the tankers had carried through the village with lightning speed. The villagers came running and crowded around. An additional two plows appeared. We set off to assemble some kind of harness.

The blacksmith shop became the center of the village's life for the evening and almost the entire night. All the remaining *Emchisti* left their vehicles to help in the work: they burned an enormous bush to make charcoal for the forge; they dragged in the tank tow cables to be modified for the plows. Several young women helped. And soon the rhythmic pounding of the blacksmith's hammer was heard. Forging began. Oksana held a small, long-handled hammer in her hand and adroitly pointed with it where the "smithy"—Senior Sergeant Gennadiy Kapranov—was to strike.

The tankers, admiring the coordinated work of their comrade and the village girl, joked, "A soldier is always a soldier—in any endeavor, he is a go-getter!" "Oksana is a blacksmith—is she any less amazing?" replied the villagers with pride.

The heated red hot strip of metal was transformed before our eyes into simple parts and components of the future harnesses. Although the "smithies" were replaced, Oksana stood as before near the anvil. The crude harnesses were ready by dawn. The village women were not sleeping in their homes either. From their meager supplies they cooked, roasted, and baked, preparing the soldiers' breakfast. Though they were not rich, they gave from their hearts.

After three hours of heavy sleep, the entire "tank field brigade" was on its feet. The indefatigable Oksana led the *Emchisti* to a half-destroyed school building. There they found a table set for the breakfast meal. They ate fried eggs with lard, pancakes with cracklings, and washed it all down with compote [stewed fruit]. Having thanked the cooks for the tasty meal, the tankers acknowledged with laughter, "Now we are ready to take the bull by the horns, and plow more than the gardens!"

The exhaust noise of tank engines echoed over Chernovtsy. One Sherman behind the houses on the right side of the road, the other on the left, attacked the garden plots. The driver-mechanics steered their vehicles with great care. Would the makeshift harnesses pull the load? It took some time for the "farmers" to master the difficult task of handling their plows. They had to remain calm. Just a bit of hesitation, and the plowshare was gliding along the surface of the soil, scraping away only the grass. With each meter of forward progress, the driver-mechanics handled their vehicles more confidently, and the steps of those following the plows became more firm.

This unusual picture of plowing the gardens with tanks caught the attention of the villagers. Small boys, old people with skin white as the moon, stooping old women, and several young people appeared everywhere. They spilled out into the fields and quietly observed the scene.

Midday. The last furrow was laid down. The tank engines died. Quiet ruled over Chernovtsy once again. Only around the schoolhouse could be heard the sounds of happy women's voices. Preparations were under way there for a large holiday feast, the likes of which hadn't been seen in this war-torn village for more than three years.

I ordered the tankers to prepare to move out. We put the last of the diesel fuel in the Shermans and checked our tracks.

Limping heavily (she had twisted her ankle a week before), Hanna Ivanovna approached me. She embraced me firmly and we exchanged kisses. "You can't imagine what joy you have given us! You have taken a great burden from the shoulders of my villagers; in a single day they have been freed from their misfortune. Thank you so very, very much, dear soldiers of ours!" She shook hands with and kissed each tanker and invited all of us and the villagers to come to the table. The crews closed the hatches on their Emchas and headed for the school.

We were party to many and various meals on our long wartime journey. But this was one of the most memorable, one that has stayed with me all these years. It was not a particular dish, not the strength or quantity of the prepared food. It was the atmosphere of the meal and especially the tears.

I had been in the active army for more than a year. In the Smolensk area, in Byelorussia, I had seen boundless grief. Totally burned-out cities and villages. As they counted up after the war, every fourth inhabitant of Byelorussian territory had perished. A river of human tears flowed there.

But in Chernovtsy, a rural Ukrainian village, for the first time during the war we witnessed the bright, happy tears of old peasants, thanking us for our "good work." Tears of joy. We cannot possibly forget their deep (all the way to the ground) bows.

The Shermans departed to the west. Young and old gathered at the village outskirts. They accompanied the unexpected plowmen to the main road leading to the front. They discreetly made the sign of the cross. Gennadiy Kapranov and several other young men promised to return to this village after the war's end. They were attracted to the Ukrainian pony tails. But their secret fantasies were never realized. They were buried in single and common graves in the cities, villages, and fields of Romania, Hungary, Czechoslovakia, and Austria. May they rest in peace!

Retribution

In the last days of March 1944, the motorized infantry and tank units of the 5th Mechanized Corps forced the Prut River and captured a bridgehead on its right [western] bank. The front line had stabilized. We, the tankers of the 233d Brigade, along with the infantry, had to hold our positions for nearly two weeks. During this time, we did not receive fresh replacements.

At the moment of its arrival at the Soviet-Romanian border, the brigade had a significant shortage of Sherman tanks. It received the mission to defend a sector on the right side of the highway leading into Jassy. Our units were opposed by up to a battalion of enemy infantry, reinforced by several Tiger tanks. Both sides positioned their armored combat vehicles almost at the forward edge, significantly strengthening the antitank defense of the infantry. Both we and the Germans prepared our positions well. Only the tops of the turrets were visible.

With the appearance of heavy German tanks on the Soviet-German front, we were confronted with their unusual external rigging. Track blocks were hung on the front slope of the hull and along the entire turret. In the first place, this reinforced the armor defenses of the Tigers and Panthers. Second, an armor-piercing round that struck one of these fixtures was normally deflected.

The front-line trace had an influence on the nature of the activities of the opposing sides, especially in the conduct of fire. The front-line passed rigidly from north to south. For this reason, in the morning the bright spring sun blinded the enemy and in the afternoon blinded us.

A Tiger firing position was located on the eastern slope of one of the hills. From here, its crew could overlook our position almost up to the Prut River, in particular the road to the crossing site. Good observation and fire control optics of the "beast" and the long-range 88-mm cannon permitted the Germans to conduct precise fire on any target, large or small. For example, after 1300, anything that appeared on the road was quickly destroyed. "Rabid Fritz," as our soldiers christened it, did not experience any shortage of high-explosive shells.

We could not respond to the enemy with similar activities for a number of reasons. Because of the hilliness, we could see only a short distance into his defenses. We also had to conserve ammunition. Our own supply system had not yet caught up with us. How we wanted to get revenge on "Rabid Fritz." The impatience of the Emchisti, finally, was overextended when they had to go without fresh hot meals for two straight days. The cooks were driven off and had to send food forward in thermal containers.

Senior Sergeant Anatoliy Romashkin had already given much thought to the problem of how to punish the unleashed bully. After this incident, the gun commander firmly cemented his fame as a precise gunner. The circumstances once again urgently called for confirmation of the rank and recognition accorded him by his comrades. Anatoliy scratched his head for more than a day on the practical accomplishment of the planned retribution. He constantly observed the movements of the enemy crew. He determined the range to the Tiger with careful precision—650 meters.

The retribution was prepared and carried out in the following manner.

Romashkin received permission to fire two antitank rounds. He requested the infantry commander to assign him a sniper. With the sniper's assistance, Romashkin selected a firing position near his tank, from which the entire turret of the Tiger could be easily seen. Anatoliy recommended that the sniper, Junior Sergeant Yuriy Prokhorov, fire armor-piercing ammunition [such as would be used to disable a light-skinned vehicle] because it had a heavier propellant charge. "I might have to expend both main gun rounds. You should hit the target with the first shot."

Over the course of two days, from dawn to 1300, while the sun was not shining in their eyes, Anatoliy and Yuriy vigilantly tracked the beast. But no luck. The other men, not knowing the reason for the postponement of the intended payback, teased Romashkin. He remained silent. Sometimes he retorted with an unintelligible, "If I don't get the angle, I don't shoot!" The essence of the gunner's plan was to wait patiently until the Tiger's main gun was pointed off five to ten degrees. He would fire from the Sherman at the Tiger's gun tube. But all this time, it stared at us with its threatening muzzle brake. With such a small target area, the probability of destroying the "88" approached zero.

The third day of waiting began. A light morning fog was dissipating. Anatoliy put his eye to the sight. His heart leaped with joy. "Finally!" He immediately gave the prearranged signal to Yuriy. "Prepare to fire!" One second, two . . . five. The turret of the beast slowly rotated. Perhaps he could catch the target. Meanwhile, the rays of the rising sun were not striking his eyes. A main gun shot from the Emcha tore through the air. Identified by its tracer, the round, slamming against the turret mantle, had gone right and up. Another shot. This one struck home! Like a sawed log, almost half of the Tiger's gun tube flew off to the side. The cupola hatch immediately opened with a clank—the enemy tank commander raised himself out almost to the waist. Anatoliy saw in his gunsight how even the German's mouth fell open in surprise at the sight of the remaining stub of his long gun [main gun tube].

Prokhorov squeezed the trigger of his sniper rifle. The German jerked and then fell face downward on the turret roof. "Ura-a-a!" The shouts rang out over our positions. "The 'maniac' has been shot!" Romashkin humbly reported.

The wounded Tiger withdrew to the rear of the German position with the coming of darkness. From this time forward, nothing replaced it on the hill. The crews of other beasts became "quieter than water, lower than grass." The front-line road now was traveled in daylight. Sometimes, true, it was subjected to artillery fire and the occasional air strike.

The Secret Firm

Time has inexorably moved on. We—foreign-vehicle tankers—have grown fewer and fewer in number. As in the past, we wartime comrades gather for a commemoration twice each year, on 9 May—Victory Day—and on the second Sunday in September—the Day of Armored Forces.

As is well known, the majority of the Lend-Lease combat equipment was delivered to the Soviet Union by maritime convoys. It was offloaded in Murmansk or Arkhangel'sk and then was transported by rail to its destination. The Shermans that we received were carefully covered with a thick, dark, impregnated paper. Only the driver-mechanic's hatch was left untreated. The driver's compartment had to be accessible because the tank moved under its own power from the port to the rail-loading station.

Almost two days were required to remove this "skin" from the Emcha. I have to give the Americans their due. The machines were excellently prepared for their long journey by sea. During my time at the front, I received new Sherman tanks on five occasions. And never, when removing the shipping and packing preparations, did I find even a drop of moisture in the crew compartment. I know they spent more than a day or two at sea.

At the end of March 1944, the 233d Tank Brigade received replacement personnel and combat vehicles. We received the arriving group of eight Emchas on 8 April at Bel'tsy station. We drove them at night to the village of Skulyany, where the brigade's 1st and 2d Battalions were deployed. On the following day, we set about removing the wrappers from the tanks. In the morning, Misha (the American technical representative with corps headquarters) arrived at the brigade location. He silently observed our efforts for several minutes. The crews were trying to remove the "black undershirt" from the Shermans without damaging the paint on the hull and turret. We managed to accomplish this. Misha was satisfied with the results of our difficult work. Then he posed an interesting question. Did we find any small food parcels in the tanks from the workers who had assembled the vehicles? It turned out that in this case, the parcels had disappeared somewhere between the offloading port and our receipt of the tanks at the railhead. Misha was quite distressed. We had seen him in this state when the Emchas had slid around on the icy road near Fastov in Ukraine.

During the unpacking of the Sherman, much effort, some of it very intricate, was required on the part of the gunner. The main gun and the machine guns (coaxial and hull-mounted) were abundantly covered with thick grease [cosmoline]. The gun tube with muzzle brake and breach components were liberally packed with gun grease (the removal of these 25- to 30-cm plugs required some effort).

The operation to put the long gun in working order normally began with the removal of the grease from its outer surface. This was not a particularly difficult process. Cleaning the grease out of the bore was another matter entirely. Simple devices were used for this task: wooden trowels, staffs, and sticks of various lengths and configurations. The muzzle end of the gun tube was cleaned out first. The breach grease plug was pushed into the crew compartment with a ramming staff inserted at the muzzle. This chore sometimes required the effort of two or three crew members. Our men began this process with the first of the several "Americans" received by the brigade.

Work proceeded in sequence. On one of the Shermans of Yakushkin's company, cleaning of the main gun tube was nearing completion. Then, suddenly, something totally unexpected occurred. Along with two grease plugs, a bottle of whiskey, wrapped in a plastic sheet, crashed onto the floor of the crew compartment and broke. What a surprise! The tank commander, Viktor Akulov, was speechless. After a few seconds, the happy alarm was sounded from one end of the street to the other, "Stop! Stop! Stop punching gun tubes!"

A sequence of tasks was developed in the company for removing the gun tube parcels. After removal of the grease plug at the muzzle brake, a thin staff was used to carefully dislodge the middle barrier, then the gun tube was gingerly depressed at the muzzle. A shelter half or tarpaulin was held at the muzzle to receive the gift. The catch was made. How thoughtfully and cleverly this mini-gift was packed so it did not rattle around inside the bore. And it remained intact. In fact, during transport, just as on the march, the Sherman's main gun tube was fastened into a travel lock. It was depressed a bit and immobilized by a device mounted on the front slope of the tank's hull.

We immediately decided to maintain the secrecy of the "secret firm." The foreign-vehicle tankers preserved this secret until the last days of the war.

On his second day in the battalion, Misha came roaring up to us. He was radiant, happy. "The factories are good! Some time ago I informed them about your failure to receive the gifts. They have found a good place to hide their presents!"

A "Cocktail" for the Shermans

The Jassy-Kishinev strategic offensive operation (20 to 29 August 1944) was conducted by forces of the Second and Third Ukrainian *Fronts*, in coordination with the Black Sea Fleet and the Danube River Flotilla.

The purpose of this operation was to defeat the enemy on the Jassy-Kishinev axis, liberate Moldavia, and effect the departure of Romania from the war on the side of fascist Germany. By the beginning of the operation, forces of the Second Ukrainian *Front*, commanded by Army General R. Ya. Malinovskiy, and Third Ukrainian *Front*, commanded by Army General F. I. Tolbukhin, were positioned at the line Krasnoilsk–Pashkani, north of Jassy, farther along the Dniester River to the Black Sea.

The German command was striving at any cost to hold Romania in the fascist coalition, as its principal supplier of petroleum (half of all German oil was from Romania), as a supply base (from 1939 to 1944, 1.4 million tons of grain were received from Romania, along with human resources), and as a shield in the Balkans. Therefore, a relatively strong grouping of German and Romanian forces remained here.

Army Group South Ukraine, consisting of the Eighth and Sixth German and Fourth Romanian Armies, and the XVII Separate

German Corps were defending opposite the Second and Third Ukrainian *Fronts*. These formations comprised forty-seven divisions and five brigades.

The enemy, taking advantage of the mountainous terrain and the countless water obstacles, had created an engineer-reinforced defense, echeloned to a depth of eighty kilometers. It included three, and on the Jassy axis, four defensive lines. Defensive lines had also been constructed in the depths of the enemy's defense, along the Prut and Siret rivers. The enemy's main forces (Sixth Army of fifteen divisions, of which fourteen were German) stood in the center of the operational formation of Army Group South Ukraine, on the Kishinev axis, and Romanian forces were defending on the flanks.

The Soviet command skillfully employed the favorable configuration of the front line and the weak support on the flanks of the enemy grouping. By the concept of the operation, forces of the Second and Third Ukrainian *Fronts* were to break through enemy defenses from remote and opposite areas (northwest of Jassy and south of Bender) and, developing success along conjoining axes at Husi, Vaslui, and Felchiu, surround and destroy the main body of Army Group South Ukraine. The subsequent mission was to develop the offensive into the depth of Romania at a high tempo.

Both *fronts* had a combined strength of ninety [rifle] divisions and six tank and mechanized corps. Soviet forces outnumbered the enemy 1.4:1 in infantry, 2:1 in artillery, 4.7:1 in tanks and self-propelled guns, and 2.7:1 in aircraft.[1]

The commander of the Second Ukrainian *Front* decided to break through the enemy's tactical zone in a sixteen-kilometer sector between the Jassy and Tyrgu-Frumos fortified regions with forces of the 27th and 52d Armies. The 6th Tank Army and 18th Tank Corps were to be committed on the first day of the operation after the breakthrough of the tactical defensive zone along Mare ridge by the combined arms armies and, attacking toward Larga, Vaslui, and Felchiu, reach the line Bacau-Husi by the close of the second day. Together with the forces of the Third Ukrainian *Front*, they were to encircle the enemy Jassy-Kishinev grouping. Subsequently, a large portion of the force—thirty-one rifle divisions, one mechanized corps, two tank corps, and one cavalry corps—was to develop the offensive on the external encirclement front toward Focsani and Transylvania. The other portion of the forces—seventeen rifle divisions and one tank corps—in cooperation with the Third Ukrainian *Front,* was to destroy the encircled enemy force. It was decided to conduct a supporting attack in the direction of Roman with the 7th Guards Army and a cavalry-mechanized group to support the shock group from the Carpathian Mountain side.

The selected axis of the main attack was aimed at the most vulnerable spot—the seam between the Fourth Romanian and Eighth German Armies, which was defended primarily by Romanian forces, and where there were no permanent fortifications. This axis was the shortest route to crossings on the Prut River, into the rear of the German Sixth Army.

A uniqueness of the breakthrough plan along the sector of the Second Ukrainian *Front* was that infantry formations on the main attack axis were not only to break through the enemy tactical zone on the first day of the offensive but also to support the introduction of the 6th Tank Army into the rupture.

Two phases of the offensive were planned for the Second Ukrainian *Front.* In the first phase, the forces of this *front* and the Third Ukrainian *Front* were to join together and then achieve a penetration of up to 100 kilometers in depth with their combined arms armies. The average daily rate of advance for rifle divisions was figured at twenty kilometers and for mobile forces at forty to forty-five kilometers. In the second phase, forces were to participate in the liquidation of the encircled enemy grouping and simultaneously pursue the enemy in the direction of Focsani to a depth of 220 to 230 kilometers.

On the evening of 19 August, reconnaissance by battle was conducted by forces of both *fronts.* These activities established that the enemy was occupying forward defensive positions and showed no indication of withdrawing.

On the morning of 20 August, after a powerful artillery and, on the sector of the Third Ukrainian *Front,* aerial bombardment, the *fronts'* assault forces launched their offensives.

Forces of the 27th Army, Second Ukrainian *Front,* broke through the enemy's main defensive belt within three hours and by 1200 to 1300 had forced the Bakhlui River. They broke into the enemy's second defensive belt from the march. At 1400, the corps of the 6th Tank Army were committed in the offensive zone of the 27th Army. By evening, the tank army's formations, supported by aviation, had reached the enemy's third defensive belt, which was situated along the Mare ridge. The corps of the 6th Tank Army and 27th Army were unable to break through this defensive belt.

On the morning of 21 August, the 18th and 23d Tank Corps were committed. In twenty-four hours of intensive fighting, the forces of the Second Ukrainian *Front* broke through all three enemy defensive belts to a depth of thirty kilometers, developing a breach sixty-five kilometers wide along the front. Favorable conditions developed for intensive pursuit of the enemy and the encirclement of his Jassy-Kishinev grouping.

The 6th Tank Army, advancing on four axes in a zone from twenty-four to fifty kilometers wide, at a rate of thirty to thirty-five kilometers per day, broke into the town of Vaslui on the evening of 22 August and by the evening of 23 August reached the area of Bîrlad. The 18th Tank corps was fighting near Husi.

Over the course of five days, forces of the Second and Third Ukrainian *Fronts* had encircled a large enemy grouping—the German Sixth Army. Eighteen divisions had been caught in the "bag." In the second phase of the Jassy-Kishinev operation, the Soviet command designated thirty-four divisions for the internal front to liquidate the surrounded enemy force and employed the main forces of the Second and Third Ukrainian *Fronts* (more than fifty divisions, including the 6th Tank Army) for developing the offensive on the external front, deep into Romania.

By the close of 27 August, encircled enemy forces east of the Prut River had been liquidated, and on 29 August, units that had managed to cross the Prut River west of Husi suffered the same fate. Altogether, twenty-two German divisions and almost all the Romanian formations that were at the front had been destroyed.

From 20 to 29 August 1944, units of the 5th Mechanized Corps of the 6th Tank Army participated in the Jassy-Kishinev offensive operation as part of the Second Ukrainian *Front*. During this time, the *Emchisti* covered a distance of 350 kilometers. The offensive developed with a tempo of from 35 to 75 kilometers per twenty-four-hour period. The gap between tank units and combined arms formations sometimes reached 60 to 80 kilometers.

In such rapidly unfolding and intense battles, the Sherman was subjected to an all-encompassing and severe trial, the likes of which it would never have experienced in the most thorough test environment. The experience was doubly hard on the crews. They bent, but they did not break. The situation forced all categories of officers to make exceptionally cogent and, on occasion, risky decisions.

The 233d Tank Brigade, along with other corps units, was committed to the fight on the afternoon of 20 August. Overcoming stubborn enemy resistance, by the end of the day the forces had penetrated into the enemy's third defensive belt that passed along the Mare ridge. Fierce battles continued throughout the night. On the morning of the following day, brigade units began a rapid movement in the direction of Vaslui [fifty kilometers south of Jassy, Romania] and beyond to Bîrlad. During this time, a rather complex situation was developing in the rear of the attacking formations. A portion of the German-fascist forces that had been surrounded northeast of Khushi [twenty-five kilometers east of Vaslui] had broken out of the "ring" and, moving in a southwestward direction, had cut all the roads leading to the front line. Several of our logistic facilities and headquarters had been destroyed. Troubling news reached us. We could not count on any timely resupply of fuel or ammunition! Meanwhile, the command was demanding that we increase the tempo of our own attack— there was an uprising in Bucharest. We had little ammunition for the infantry weapons, one-half of the specified norm of main gun rounds, and our diesel fuel was exhausted. In a word, the picture was bleak.

The 233d Brigade eliminated two infantry battalions on the approaches to Bîrlad that had the mission to set up a defense at a good position to cover the town from the north. We captured some good booty: weapons and food. Senior Lieutenant Ivan Yakushkin ordered each *tankodesantnik* to arm himself with a German submachine gun, in addition to his own PPSh.[2] Each soldier was also to take three hundred rounds for his German weapon and conserve his own ammunition.

This imaginative decision by the commander of the 1st Tank Company became known throughout the battalion and, in a brief time, in other brigade units as well. "A good idea spreads to the world!" It reflected the spirit of commanders of various ranks.

One vexing problem had been resolved. Another no less important issue remained—fuel. We searched for diesel fuel in

Bîrlad. There was gasoline and some kerosene, but no diesel. The Shermans were draining the last liters from their fuel cells. Ivan Yakushkin made the following suggestion to Major Grigoriy Gorodilov, the battalion commander. He recommended we prepare a "cocktail" for the Emchas from the available fuels, a measure of gasoline mixed with two measures of kerosene, and test it on one tank.

We filled the tank of Junior Lieutenant Konstantin Stepanov with such a mixture. The Sherman made a three-kilometer circle, with reassuring results. The motor overheated a bit, requiring more frequent stops during movement to cool the diesel motor.

An appropriate order was issued. We all refueled. When all the main fuel cells were topped off, we filled our auxiliary drums. Forward! Forward! On to Bucharest! The Romanian "cocktail" did not let us down. Our tanks accomplished the assigned mission.

The Yakushkin Method

Immediately before the Jassy-Kishinev operation, we received a shipment of Shermans in the brigade that lacked large-caliber antiaircraft machine guns. We sorely missed these weapons in the fierce August-September battles.

After Bîrlad, the tanks of the 233d Brigade surged southward toward the "Focsani gates" (mountains on the west, river on the east [114 kilometers southwest of Vaslui]). If it was at all possible, we had to get there in a hurry. The Germans understood our intentions well. They fell upon the brigade units with air strikes. We had nothing with which to ward off the airplanes.

It was the morning of 25 August and already the third air raid. Two tanks had been damaged and one wheeled vehicle set afire in Ivan Yakushkin's company. Ivan Ignat'evich was upset and pensive. He assembled his platoon and tank commanders and the commander of the tankodesantniki. They conducted a careful analysis of the actions of their subordinates during the enemy air attacks. It was noted that some crews halted their vehicles during an immediate threat of air attack. "This is a big mistake. It is more difficult for the enemy to hit a moving target." The issue was posed to everyone, "How can we avoid the bombs dropped by the enemy dive-bombers?" Lacking a response, the officers were silent.

Ivan Yakushkin suggested what at first glance seemed to be an improbable course of action for the crews in such a situation. He explained his idea in some detail and even gave a practical demonstration of how to execute it. "Let's try it. I think it'll work. Right now, I don't see any other solution," the company commander said.

Upon receipt of the warning signal "Air!" two members of the crew, the tank commander and driver-mechanic, had to combine all their will into a single, coordinated effort. They had to display nerves of steel. Even now, after many years have passed, I can't help but be astonished. How did this work?

The company column was moving along a road at maximum speed. The *tankodesantniki* were sitting atop the tank, the barrels of their trophy *Schmeissers* bristling to the right and left. They were prepared to unleash heavy fire at any moment. High corn was standing on both sides of the road. Be alert! The tank commanders were standing almost waist high in their hatches, warily searching the sky.

Several kilometers of road lay behind us. We heard a loud "Air!" on our headsets. Picking up speed, the Shermans acquired some distance between vehicles, not less than one hundred meters. Everyone outside the tank jumped into the turret. It was very crowded in the tank's crew compartment, but the *tankodesantniki* were protected from machine-gun fire and bomb fragments.

The tank commander kept his hatch half open in order to track the maneuvers of the attacking aircraft. The tank intercom system passed communications only in one direction during these crucial moments—from the tank commander to the driver-mechanic.

The German bombers circled above. They had spotted a target on the ground. The decisive moment arrived. The tank commander spotted a bomb separating from the *Ju-87* [*Stuka*] aircraft diving on his vehicle. The bomb grew larger with every second of its flight. The officer, calculating the trajectory of its flight, adjusted the subsequent movement of the Sherman. A spurt forward, and the bomb fell behind the tank; a rapid drop in speed or momentary halt, and the geyser of the explosion was in front of the tank. A rush forward, and the Emcha hurriedly abandoned the danger zone.

This, of course, was a dangerous "game with death." In a majority of cases, the foreign-vehicle tankers came out of it the winners. True, our fatigues and coveralls were sweat-soaked. There was time later to wring them out. The tank commander's exceptional eyesight, will, and courage and the driver-mechanic's masterly command of the vehicle defeated the efforts of the enemy pilots.

The "Yakushkin method" (thus it was nicknamed in the brigade, a name that was carried to other corps units) was successfully employed to the end of the Great Patriotic War. All the phases of this "suicide dance" were carefully polished. Thanks to this, scores of Shermans remained combat effective.

Barefooted

During the war years, each branch of the active army had its basic slang dictionary. For example, in the 233d Tank Brigade, "sunflower seeds" were small arms cartridges; "cucumbers" were mortar shells; "overseas cucumbers" were main gun rounds for the Sherman, and so on.

At the end of August 1944, a new, unusual meaning of "barefooted" literally burst into this dictionary like a whirlwind. A radiogram bearing this word fell like a bomb on the head of the tank army command. It also caused some concern in the headquarters of the Second Ukrainian *Front*. The ensuing "hurricane" swept through various military channels in Moscow. They were saying that it would be reported to the Supreme High Commander [Stalin] himself. Perhaps. The events were extremely unusual. One could say that almost 75 percent of the foreign-made tanks of the 5th Mechanized Corps became combat ineffective in one hour. This was in the period of the successful Jassy-Kishinev operation. Our advancing forces had crossed the

Siret River from the march. After a brief and intense battle on 27 August, the Focsani fortified region, the enemy's last serious defensive line, was cracked open. Tanks of the mechanized corps moved into a clean operational expanse. Our logistics, finally, caught up with forward units. The troops lacked nothing now. "There are no problems beyond the Siret River!"

August of 1944 was very hot in Romania. Not a drop of rain. The main highway was a scorching frying pan. The secondary roads were dust bowls. The fields had deep cracks in them.

The tank brigade was in the second week of a frenzied offensive. The driver-mechanics and their assistants were having a particularly difficult time. Commanders tried to give them two or three hours of sleep on the floor of the crew compartment. The other crew members were not permitted this luxury. If they were able, they could catch a few winks at their crew stations.

The "birthday" of the great panic was 28 August. It was on this day that someone said, "We will soon be barefooted." This code word quickly made the rounds through the rumor mill and in written documents. The track system of the Sherman became the cause of serious concern. In comparison to the T-34, it had a much more complex construction. Three suspension bogies were mounted on each side of the Emcha, each with two fore and aft rubber-lined road wheels. On the seventh day of this forced march, cracks began to appear in the rubber of the road wheels. The rubber could not withstand the constant heavy overheating. At the first opportunity, the crews poured water over them. Not even a single drop of "nature's call" was wasted. None of the preventive measures we took made any difference. On the following day, chunks of rubber began to cover the road's surface. The Emchas became more and more "barefooted" with each passing kilometer. By the end of the day, the road wheels were completely stripped of rubber. The metal track passed over metal wheels, resulting in a unique creaking, scraping noise. This unbelievable cacophony could be heard for kilometers around. One couldn't even think about concealing the brigade's actions. As soon as our plight became known, the same misfortune was visited upon other corps units. The corps' principal striking force—its tanks— were basically worn out.

We continued our "squeaking offensive" for almost another

day. The engines overheated on the Shermans with bare road wheels. On 30 August, on the approaches to Bucharest, the "barefooted" were given the command to halt.

By evening, they had brought up new road wheels. They say they were delivered by aircraft from Moscow itself. For three days, the crews, along with the brigade, corps, and army maintenance personnel, re-tired the Emchas. Then a new forced march to the north, into Transylvania.

An Unbelievable Event

If one took the conditions that existed when this incident occurred, designed a program, and did the necessary calculations with the most modern computer, I am firmly convinced that the result would be negative. Such an event would be deemed impossible. Just the same, the unbelievable happened.

In early October 1944, the 1st Tank Battalion, 46th Guards (formerly 233d) Brigade, had reached the approaches to the city of Turda (northern Transylvania [on the Ar'esh River just north of its juncture with the Muresh River]). The Germans greeted us with well-organized fires of all types. Our attack was halted. The Shermans ended up in a harvested cornfield. The crews camouflaged their vehicles with various makeshift materials but did not dig them in. They understood that we would not be delayed at this position for long.

Major Grigoriy Gorodilov, the battalion commander, was summoned to the brigade commander. I—the chief of staff—remained at the unit as the senior officer. It was approaching noon. Senior Lieutenant Aleksandr Kuchma, commander of the 2d Tank Company, taking advantage of the lull between battles, decided to listen to the latest news on the radio at 1200. He normally wrote down the interesting events and later informed his subordinates. He always did this when the opportunity presented itself to pull in the station on his vehicle radio.

Aleksandr lowered himself into the combat compartment of the Emcha. The tank's radio was mounted in the lower rear portion of the turret. To reach the radio more conveniently, he elevated the gun tube a bit [thus lowering the breach] and dropped the spent cartridge bag.[1] He turned on the radio. With his back against the breach of the main gun, he placed his notebook on the tank commander's seat and prepared to record the news. Moscow's call sign was already sounding in the headphones. At this time, the radio operator, Guards Sergeant Nikolay Shevtsov, who was standing radio watch at the shortwave receiver, was in the turret with the commander. Therefore, he was both a witness to and a victim of the tragedy that occurred.

The first thing that the sergeant remembered clearly was a bright shell burst, the whistle of fragments in the turret, and a burning hot pain in his left arm. Then Nikolay saw the company commander slowly slipping down to the turret floor. Before this, Shevtsov had squatted down for a moment to move two main gun rounds out of the way. They normally stood on the floor of the turret, but they were in Lieutenant Kuchma's way.

Having forgotten about his own wound, the radio operator quickly picked up the unconscious officer. Warm streams of blood flowed onto Nikolay's palms. "The commander is wounded!" Shevtsov cried with all his strength. At that time, other members of the crew were lying under the tank. A German reconnaissance aircraft had appeared over our position. Everyone who was outside the vehicle had taken cover under the Sherman. Several seconds earlier, the German aircraft had made a low-level pass, and strafed the battalion's combat formation with his aircraft cannon.

The alarm spread: "Senior Lieutenant Kuchma is wounded!" I ran toward the tank of the 2d Company commander. When I approached his Emcha, I saw the crew carefully placing Aleksandr on a tarpaulin, unfolded alongside their vehicle. He was unconscious. Nikolay Shevtsov sat on the ground nearby, leaning against a road wheel. They were bandaging his wounded arm. The battalion physician's assistant [feldsher] and medics ran up and began to administer first aid to Kuchma. I ordered the battalion communications chief, Guards Senior Lieutenant Aleksandr Morshnev, to call for an ambulance from the brigade medical platoon. The company commander and radio operator had to be evacuated to a medical treatment facility.

Shevtsov reported to me about what had occurred inside the

Emcha's turret. The battalion chief of armaments, Guards Senior Lieutenant Ivan Korchak, detected the base portion of an enemy 20-mm aircraft cannon round on the turret floor. This raised the perplexing question, "How did this get into the Sherman's turret?"

While we waited for the arrival of the ambulance, we began to investigate. Which of the tank hatches were open when the company commander was in the tank? It turned out that only the commander's hatch, on the roof of the turret, was open. This was strange. Kuchma's entrance wound was between the shoulder blades, the exit wound in the lower part of his chest. Consequently, the trajectory of the aviation projectile was inclined to the horizontal. Had it fallen through the commander's hatch, the projectile would have had a near vertical trajectory. Time passed, and we did not discover the answer. A half-track ambulance brought brigade medics forward.[2] Not more than twenty minutes had passed since Kuchma had been wounded. Aleksandr Terent'evich died without having regained consciousness. We hardened veterans, who had seen many deaths on the battlefield, were deeply touched by the death of our remarkable fellow officer and faithful comrade. Meanwhile, the cause that led to such a tragic end remained a mystery. Therefore, we had to get to the bottom of it to prevent it from happening again.

Korchak and several other officers carefully inspected and probed every square centimeter of the tank turret's interior and exterior walls. They did not find any signs of the strike of an enemy projectile on the armor. There also was not the slightest crack between the Emcha's hull and turret through which a projectile could have entered the crew compartment. "Where did it come from?" This problem continued to concern every tanker.

And suddenly, amid the mournful quiet, arose the sharp exclamation of Ivan Korchak: "I found it!" Everyone who was standing with bared heads around Sasha Kuchma rushed over to the chief of armaments. And here was his explanation.

Aleksandr Terent'evich, upon lowering himself into the turret, had raised the main gun ten to fifteen degrees. Because of the way it was parked, the bow of the Sherman was already somewhat higher than the stern. As a result, the muzzle brake was now pointed at the sky. We had a standard procedure in tank forces: when a vehicle occupied a battle position, its breach was always open. Two rounds stood in the ready rack on the floor of the turret—an antitank round and a high-explosive round. Depending on which type of enemy target appeared, the gun commander gave the command to the loader: "Load antitank (high explosive)!" When the round was loaded, he fired the shot.

Two circumstances led to the mortal wounding of Kuchma: the significant elevation angle of the main gun and the open breach. It turned out that the 20-mm aviation projectile went into the bore of the elevated 76.2-mm tank main gun, passed through it, and, having encountered an obstacle—the back of the company commander leaning against the breach—detonated. The indisputable evidence of the axis of flight was the traces of the copper driving band of the enemy round on the lands of the Emcha's main gun.

This was, indeed, the truth. Unbelievable, but true.

A Daring Raid

On 5 December 1944, after a brief pause, the forces of the center of the Second Ukrainian *Front* renewed the offensive from the area of Hatvan in a general northwest direction. The intent was to go around the east side of Budapest. The 6th Guards Tank Army was committed on the afternoon of that day. At first the tankers were unable to develop a rapid tempo of advance, but they surged forward on the night of 6 December. The 9th Guards Mechanized Corps reached the bulge at Galgaguta, and the 5th Guards Tank Corps captured Acsa [approximately thirty miles northeast of Budapest].

Overcoming stubborn enemy resistance, units of the 9th Mechanized Corps developed the attack into the depth of the enemy's defenses, toward the town of Šahy [due north of Budapest on the Czech border]. At the same time, the 5th Corps broke through toward the city of Vac. The result was a sort of "scissors." Between the two corps remained an enemy grouping, which at any moment could have consolidated its strength and struck a blow against the flanks of the attacking Soviet forces. Tactical intelligence became exceptionally important in these conditions. On 12 December, the brigades of the mechanized corps, defeating enemy counterattacks, slowly moved toward Šahy and by the close of this day reached the outskirts of the town. The command of the 46th Guards Tank Brigade was interested in information on the enemy in the area southwest of Šahy. The mission was assigned to the brigade's scouts. The chief of staff of the 1st Battalion, Guards Captain Nikolay Bogdanov, was ordered to conduct a daring raid into the zone of Bernesebarat and Kemence. Captain Bogdanov chose to conduct this raid on a Sherman tank.

Two circumstances, Nikolay Nikolayevich asserted, would assist him in accomplishing this task. First, the enemy's defense in this sector had been created hurriedly. Only built-up areas along the roads had been prepared for defense. The terrain between them was considered impassable during this time of the year, even on foot. Hardly a thought had been given to armored equipment. But this was exactly how Bogdanov planned to penetrate into the enemy rear—on a tank. The low ground pressure of the Emcha permitted him to engage in such a risky venture.

Second, the captain's excellent knowledge of German would play a decisive role in his accomplishment of the mission. The suggested scenario for Nikolay Nikolayevich's actions went something like this. He and a driver-mechanic would dress in German uniforms. They would take with them an additional two crewmen—a gunner and a loader. These two personnel would remain inside the turret and not expose themselves. They would maintain the tank's weapons in constant readiness to open fire.

The brigade command, acknowledging the many favorable combat qualities of these *gvardeytsi* [guardsmen], gave their approval to this unusual tank reconnaissance, to be conducted on the night of 13 December. It was raining steadily, at times turning into snow. There is an old saying about this kind of weather: "A good master does not send his dog outside."

The commander of the 1st Battalion, Guards Captain Ivan Yakushkin, understood the risk that Bogdanov was taking. Ivan Ignat'evich felt it necessary to remind his chief of staff of already proven courses of action: during the approach to any objective in the enemy's rear, if the situation permitted, sneak up on one motor. The Emcha could crawl like a cat. Stay on the downwind side, and use the radio only in the most extreme emergency.

The author in Hungary, March 1945, at the rank of Guards Captain.
(*Courtesy of the author*)

Captain Nikolay Maslyukov, commander of the 1st Battalion until his death in late January 1944. (*Courtesy of the author*)

Shermans of the 1st Battalion, 46th Guards Tank Brigade, on the streets of Vienna, April 1945. On the side armor of the lead tank are written the words "For the Motherland!" The two-legged device mounted on the front slope in front of the driver and immediately below the main gun tube is the travel lock, used to secure the main gun during nontactical movement of the vehicle. (*Courtesy of "Planeta" Publishing House*)

A Soviet mortar crew deploys forward during the battle for the center of Vienna, as a Sherman tank provides overwatch. (*Courtesy of "Planeta" Publishing House*)

An American-manufactured scout car, mounting a Browning M-2.50 caliber machine gun, advances with infantry along the streets of Vienna. (*Courtesy of "Planeta" Publishing House*)

After the battle, Viennese women make their way past a Sherman tank and an American-manufactured truck. (*Courtesy of author*)

Guards Captain D. F. Loza (left) and his father, Private Fedor Loza, meet for the first time after the victory in Europe at a railroad station in Siberia. (*Courtesy of the author*)

Guards Senior Lieutenant Dmitriy Niyakiy, one of Loza's two subordinate company commanders in the Far East. (*Courtesy of the author*)

1st Battalion chief of staff, Guards Captain N. Bogdanov (left) and one of the battalion's platoon commanders, Guards Lieutenant Mikhail Golubev. (*Courtesy of the author*)

A Sherman makes its way across a causeway reinforced by cut logs, as
half-naked Soviet infantry and sappers look on. (*Courtesy of the author*)

The Sherman has advanced beyond the log road but remains in a foot or
more of water. (*Courtesy of "Planeta" Publishing House*)

Unable to negotiate the railroad bridge because of its narrow sides, this Sherman has just forded a stream and is climbing out on the far side. Note the self-recovery log secured to the left side of the vehicle and the fuel drums stowed on the back deck. (*Courtesy of the author*)

This advice was important. German radio intelligence constantly monitored our communications channels and quickly homed in on the position of the source of radio transmissions.

The Sherman's motors hummed quietly. It slipped off into the darkness at a slow speed. Bogdanov had in his hands a 1:100,000 German topographic map. One centimeter equaled one kilometer. It was a good, detailed map. The Germans were very familiar with the territory of their Hungarian vassal. The tank proceeded along a woodline, in freshly fallen shallow snow, that extended along the western slopes of the Berzhen hills. Nikolay Nikolayevich had chosen this route for a reason—it was deserted. There were no villages along it, only fields and thickets. After moving ahead five kilometers, he turned the Emcha ninety degrees and drove westward, and later northward, to approach the target area from the rear. In this rapidly changing situation that frequently was obscure to the enemy, such an approach would perhaps bring success.

The weather worsened. The wind blew wet snow into their faces. It was coming out of the north, through the "tunnel" between the Gron River and the Berzhen hills. They maintained their course using the tank's gyrocompass. Soon they should come upon the highway that ran between Bernesebarat and Kemence. His watch was showing 2200 Moscow time. Finally, they reached the hardstand and increased speed. A little more than a mile down the road, Bogdanov spotted the dark silhouette of an enemy armored vehicle on the road. He ordered his driver-mechanic, Guards Senior Sergeant Mikhail Bolotin, to stop. Bogdanov jumped down to the ground. Not hurrying, he approached the enemy machine. In an authoritative tone of voice, he called out to the crew. A hatch opened on the turret. One, then a second, head appeared. Bogdanov asked, "Where are the rest of the tanks?" They explained that only the two of them remained in the self-propelled gun. Their engine had broken down, and the commander and two other crewmen had gone to the headquarters in Kemence.

Nikolay Nikolayevich went around the left side of the self-propelled gun. His spirits soared. A week ago, a small advance guard of the brigade had suddenly attacked the village of Erdetarcha at night. The enemy was caught totally by surprise and offered no resistance to the attacking column. Two self-propelled guns were parked next to the church in the village, but they remained silent. The Germans had abandoned their equipment in flight for their own lives. The 1st Battalion passed through Erdetarcha in a rush, without a thought for these two self-propelled guns. They were to have been set afire later. This was an inexcusable mistake. For some reason, the brigade's following unit was delayed a bit. The enemy regained his senses, starting with the self-propelled gun crews. They returned to their recently abandoned machines and occupied their combat positions. And when the Shermans of the second echelon moved into the village, the Germans caught them in an ambush. Two Emchas were set ablaze. The enemy ambush was destroyed in a lopsided firefight. On this same day, one interesting detail was revealed: the self-propelled guns had something still unknown to us—a piece of equipment for precision firing during periods of darkness. Later it received the name "night vision sight." At that time, one of the least damaged vehicles was taken from Erdetarcha and sent directly to Moscow, to a tank scientific research institute of the Ministry of Defense of the USSR. The order went out to all tank armies to capture intact and preserve any armored vehicle that was equipped with this apparatus.

The following recognition indicators were specified for these sights: an infrared searchlight, with a protective cover, was located on the upper portion of the gun of the tank or self- propelled gun. Attached to the order was a brief sketch of the night vision device and a full-frontal photograph of the self-propelled gun, in which the searchlight was clearly visible. This self-propelled gun was equipped in this way. This is why Bogdanov became so excited.

Such luck was rare! As scouts frequently said (in their own slang): "Capture a live prisoner, or capture a vital piece of equipment." And here, at one and the same time, was the possibility of capturing prisoners and experimental equipment. This was an exceptional opportunity.

The situation demanded lightning reflexes and instant, precisely considered actions. The more so because the enemy gun crewmen had begun to stare in uncertainty at the Sherman, barely recognizable in the darkness. The chief of staff realized that in just a few seconds, these two men could quickly disappear into their turret and slam shut their hatches. And then it would be no easy task to capture them. They could communicate with their own by radio, a simple task for them in this situation. This could not be permitted!

The task of utmost importance was to lure the enemy artillerymen out of their turret. Nikolay Bogdanov loudly stated his name: "I am Captain Grossman, a liaison officer of 6th Panzer Division Headquarters. I have an order for all of our troops." And he pulled some kind of paper out of his pocket and illuminated it with his flashlight. He turned to the artillerymen and, in a distinct voice, commanded: "Come here!" He gave the same order to his own driver-mechanic.

The striking figure of the "German captain" Bogdanov (about 5' 11") and his commanding voice, his stated duty position, and some kind of paper in the hands of this officer—all taken together had their effect. In seconds, the artillerymen were standing at attention in front of the chief of staff. A third "German"—Mikhail Bolotin—ran up and quietly sidled up to the left of the "captain," opposite one of the enemy soldiers.

Events unfolded with kaleidoscopic speed. Nikolay turned on the large beam of the flashlight, handed one of the artillerymen the paper, and at the same instant shone the light into both of their eyes, blinding them for seconds. "Berem!" [Take them], the "captain" commanded. And then "Ruki vverkh!" [Hands up]; not "Hende hoch!" but in Russian. This was a greater shock; it froze them; it decisively suppressed their will to resist. On this signal, two more *gvardeytsi* flew like bullets from the Emcha. The dumbstruck Germans were tied up in minutes and deposited inside the Sherman. And so the first part of this difficult mission was quickly and successfully accomplished.

The second half of the reconnaissance mission was no less complex. The chief of staff announced his decision to the *Emchisti*: "We will take the self-propelled gun in tow! We have to get off the road quickly, hide in the darkness, and get lost in the field. We have to get back to our own lines by the shortest route. We will strictly follow the main precept of the scouts: 'Never take the same road into and out of the enemy's rear!'"

A few minutes later, a tow cable connected the enemy's self-propelled gun to the Sherman. The loader sat behind the controls of the trophy machine. Bogdanov, his gunner, and the two "tongues" were in the turret of the Emcha.[1] The duties had been specified in the event of a combat engagement: the "captain" would fire the main gun, and the gunner would serve as the loader.

When he considered towing the captive back to his own position, the chief of staff was taking an enormous risk. He well knew the ground pressure of his own Emcha. From the indistinct responses of the Germans, he understood that the self-propelled gun had a somewhat higher ground pressure.

Simply stated, he began to sweat freely. They could not turn on their headlights. This task would demand enormous effort, skill, and dexterity from the driver-mechanic. He could not drive the Sherman into a hole or pile the German vehicle into a ditch or trench.

The first one hundred meters was the most difficult for the pair. They tried to pull the German vehicle straight in the tracks of the Sherman to conceal their direction of travel (it was almost impossible to recognize the signs of its track). The ruts were deep to the point that the Emcha had to use every ounce of its power. They changed the towing method and held the towed vehicle to the side of the Sherman's track. This was less strain on the engines. Thus they proceeded back to their own lines.

They began to approach the area where the forward edge might be. Nikolay Nikolayevich began to be concerned with how they might cross the front line. His own troops might fire on them, taking them for an enemy. He had to break radio silence. He quickly encoded a message: "I am returning accompanied. I am crossing the front line at (he gave the coordinates). Cover me by fire."

This daring night raid into the near enemy rear was safely concluded. Two weeks later, an Order of the Red Banner adorned the chest of Guards Captain Nikolay Bogdanov.

An Unusual Duel

By mid-December 1944, the line of the Soviet-German front had reached the southern border of Czechoslovakia, which followed the Ipel' River. The highway and railroad, which ran along the Hungarian side of the river, were squeezed between the hills and the water obstacle near the inhabited areas of Khont and Gomok. The commander of the 46th Guards Tank Brigade, Guards Lieutenant Colonel Nikolay Mikhno, decided to break through this narrow spot with a small forward detachment and capture a bridge across the river south of the city of Šahy. [The area described is approximately twenty-eight kilometers north of the Ipel' River's confluence with the Danube, northwest of Budapest.]

A company of the brigade's 1st Tank Battalion and thirty *desantniki*, mounted on the tanks, were designated to carry out this assignment. I—a senior lieutenant and deputy battalion commander—was ordered to lead this "flying" detachment.

It was the afternoon of 11 December. Isolated small white clouds floated across the sky. A battle was being fought for the northeastern portion of Dregeypalank. The detachment rushed through the center of the village at maximum speed, heading for Khont. Combat experience had demonstrated that the enemy would not give up a wide spot in the road without a fight. We were in for a tough fight.

Two Shermans from the platoon of Guards Lieutenant Fedor Dankin were sent ahead to reconnoiter. Several minutes later, the patrol commander reported: "There are Germans in Khont. They opened up on us with heavy fire." I ordered reconnaissance to halt and carefully observe the Germans, to determine their precise firing positions. When the detachment reached Khont, it would quickly conduct precision main gun and machine-gun fire on these targets. At least, this was my intention. But the situation soon required quite different actions by my detachment.

Khont was not more than seven hundred meters away. The

growing howl of aircraft motors filled the air. Minutes later, enemy airplanes appeared overhead. As soon as the aircraft pitched back to commence their attack, my detachment of tanks, one behind the other, turned off the road. We closed into a crescent-shaped quarry on the slope of a tree-covered hill and halted. In this situation, there was no way we could deploy by the "Yakushkin method." The space was too limited.

Nine Junkers circled over the river and road, but they could not drop their bombs on the tanks with any precision. More than once the enemy pilots attempted to attack from the more desired northern direction. But to no avail. The bright winter sun blinded them. Fearing a collision with a high hill, they broke off. More often than not, their bombs detonated against the railroad embankment and did our detachment no harm. Multiple attempts to set up for dive-bombing from the south also failed. The elevation of the hill and the dense woods prevented the pilots from seeing the tanks. Consequently, they could not drop their cargo of death on the selected target with any precision. The winding road and especially the spur of the hill prevented the Junkers from reaching the detachment from the east or west. Thanks to our fortunate choice of position, our Emchas were well protected. The depression in the northern hillside was a combination of nature and the hand of man.

The detachment had to continue its forward march in order to accomplish the assigned mission. Time was on the enemy's side. He could quietly bring reserves forward into Khont and continue his engineer work in this settlement to reinforce the defenses. Despite all of this, we could do nothing except wait for nightfall.

I periodically reported by radio to the brigade commander that we were halted because of enemy aircraft attacks. He was very angry and demanded that we move forward. I understood his concern and dissatisfaction with our actions, but I could not find the words to give the command to move out of cover and attack Khont. Here—at the cutting edge—it was exceedingly obvious that we would not cross even half the distance to the enemy positions before our Shermans would be destroyed or immobilized. Aviation lurked overhead, and we would unavoidably run smack into dense antitank fire from the defenders. Losses—substantial losses—were inescapable.

Guards Lieutenant Colonel Mikhno's irate voice continued to

rage over the airwaves: "Did you forget how to fight? Is this the first time that Junkers have circled over your head?" He spared no insults and used a lot of unprintable words.

I remind the reader of one of the peculiarities of radio communications in tank forces during the Great Patriotic War. All the brigade's tank radios were tuned to a single frequency. Thus the contents of my conversations with the brigade commander and his impartial accusations toward me were heard by every platoon and tank commander.

Despite their ineffectiveness, the enemy air attacks continued. A second group of *Ju-88*s arrived to replace the first, followed by a third. The aircraft circled above the detachment for ninety minutes. And we could do nothing. They accomplished one thing: they corralled us in a long-abandoned quarry in the mountain.

Then, suddenly, one Sherman raced toward the railroad embankment. By the number on the turret, I immediately identified it as Guards Lieutenant Grigoriy Verbovoy's tank. At my demand, "Stop! Go back!" he curtly answered, "Now I will teach them a thing or two!"

The German pilots quickly spotted the tank moving out of cover and pounced on it. An unusual duel commenced between one Emcha and six German bombers.

The leading Junkers completed his approach to the bomb run and went into a dive. At this moment, the driver-mechanic, Guards Sergeant Mikhail Korablin, drove the Sherman's bow up onto the high railway embankment. The long main gun tube was pointed into the sky, almost like an antiaircraft weapon. The lead aircraft continued its headlong dive. Behind him at normal intervals came the other bombers. Our hearts pounded with worry. Six in the air against one on the ground!

The second, . . . the third. . . . Aircraft inexorably closed on Verbovoy's tank. When it seemed that nothing would save the Sherman from a direct hit by a series of bombs, its main gun went off with a roar. The tank shook and then backed down slightly. The first *Ju-88* exploded in flight. The tankers' loud "Ura-a!" echoed through the forest.

The instant destruction of the leading aircraft stunned the remaining enemy pilots. They broke off in various directions, hurriedly dropped their bombs where they fell, and, turning around sharply, flew off to the northwest. Enemy aircraft did not appear

in the air the remainder of that day or in the following days.
As it became clear several days later, a rumor was circulating
among German soldiers and officers about the "super powerful
antiaircraft guns of Russian tanks."

Without hesitation, I described the exceptional bravery of
Guards Lieutenant Grigoriy Verbovoy's crew to the brigade commander.

After the battle, Verbovoy recounted to all of us the details
of his unusual duel. He had listened as the brigade commander
repeatedly cursed the forward detachment commander for pas-
sivity outside Khont, caused by the almost continuous enemy air
attacks. He wanted to do anything he could to help in such a complicated situation. He thought . . . and thought. He could think
of nothing that would permit him to engage the troublesome
enemy aircraft. During a routine visual scan of the surrounding terrain, his eye caught the railroad embankment. A thought
flashed through his mind like lightning. "Stand the tank up on its
haunches! We can shoot the airplane down with the main gun!"

Grigoriy glued himself to the gunsight. They said about him,
with deep respect: "When Grigoriy took the sight—the enemy
hardly had a chance!" Many in the 1st Tank Battalion had received such written commendations.

Fierce battles raged for two days around Khont and Gomok.
Early on the morning of 13 December, the brigade finally broke
through this checkpoint, captured the bridge across the Ipel'
River, and burst into the Czechoslovakian city of Šahy.

Know Your Azimuth!

January 1945. We were fighting round-the-clock fierce
battles with a surrounded enemy force in the Hungarian capital.[1]
The enemy had made three desperate attempts to break through
to his forces that had fallen into the ring of encirclement. On
2 January, he launched the first unexpected strike from the area
southeast of Komárom [on the Danube River, seventy-five kilo-

meters northwest of Budapest] on the general Bicske-Budapest axis. The enemy had a superiority over the Soviet forces of 1.7:1 in troops and 2.4:1 in tanks and self-propelled guns. Despite sustaining serious losses during the five-day offensive, the Germans were able to advance to a depth of twenty-five to thirty-seven kilometers on this axis.

The offensive of the Second Ukrainian *Front* played a significant role in halting this first enemy strike. In accordance with a 4 January *Stavka*[2] order, the 6th Guards Tank Army, in conjunction with the 7th Guards Combined Arms Army, launched an attack from the area of Kamenitsa [on the east side of the Gron River in Czechoslovakia, forty-five kilometers northwest of Budapest] along the northern bank of the Danube to Komárno [on the Czechoslovakian side of the Danube River from Komárom], with the mission to capture nearby river crossing sites. Our offensive would thus threaten the German formations that were straining toward encircled Budapest.

The combat actions in this operation were characterized by a series of peculiarities that did not have analogues in the past. The offensive of the units of the 9th Guards (formerly the 5th) Mechanized Corps of the tank army commenced without an artillery preparation. The breakthrough of the enemy defense was accomplished at night, in a snowstorm. The rapid penetration of our tanks into the depth of the enemy's dispositions in such complicated weather conditions was made possible by the skillful employment of gyrocompasses mounted in each Emcha. Before this, we simply paid no attention to them, regarding them as superfluous. "Their turn arrived to lead us forward!" They enabled us accurately to maintain the specified direction of the offensive in practically zero visibility conditions. The T-34 did not have such remarkable navigational instruments.

Before the beginning of this operation, we were ordered to leave gyrocompasses only on the Shermans of the battalion and company commanders. The remainder were to be removed and given to the 5th Guards Tank Corps of our tank army.[3] Help was needed: "As brother to brother!"

An intact bridge and a small bridgehead on the west bank of the river had been captured as a result of the actions of the forces in December 1944 on the Gron River [in Czechoslovakia] west of Kamenitsa. It was from this bridgehead that the 46th Guards Tank Brigade, the first echelon of the 9th Guards Mechanized Corps, was to attack.

The great difficulty in preparing the attack toward Komárno was that it required concentrating the forces in their start position in an extremely limited period of time and, of course, secretly. On the night of 4 to 5 January, the brigade executed an eighty-kilometer road march and concentrated some twenty kilometers from the forward edge of the enemy's defenses, somewhat offset from the intended breakthrough sector. This facilitated masking the axis of our intended strike from the enemy. The brigade had the mission to move into its start position (western outskirts of Kamenitsa), deploy in prebattle formation in the bridgehead with the *tankodesantniki* aboard, launch a sudden night attack to break through the enemy defenses in front of the Gron bridgehead, and, by the night of 7 January, capture crossings on the Danube.

The brigade commander, Guards Lieutenant Colonel Nikolay Mikhno, an energetic and experienced officer, conducted commanders' reconnaissance of the march route and starting positions with the commanders of subordinate and attached units. During the course of this work, they determined the quantity of engineer effort required to maintain the unhindered movement of combat and logistic vehicles. In a short period the assigned group of sappers prepared the march route. Traffic regulators were posted at isolated difficult sectors and markers that could easily be seen at night at the remaining route segments.

Important issues were also resolved at the bridgehead: the sequence in which units were to cross the bridge and the passage of our tanks through the combat formation of the defending forces. Particular attention was given to the problem of attacking at night. The forecast was for very bad weather. An azimuth was determined from the Gron bridgehead. The order was issued to the squad commanders of the *desantniki* and officers of all ranks: "Everyone must know the azimuth!" Tankers were to write this azimuth on the inside walls of their turrets; artillerymen, on the shields of their field and antiaircraft guns; *tankodesantniki*, on the stocks of their submachine guns.

The work that was conducted to prepare for the offensive permitted the brigade's units to reach Kamenitsa without delays and subsequently to accomplish, for the most part, their difficult combat mission.

I—deputy commander of the 1st Tank Battalion—was designated commander of the forward detachment. It consisted of a tank company, two platoons of *tankodesantniki*, and a battery of large-caliber antiaircraft machine guns on American armored half-tracks. The detachment's orders were to slam into the enemy's defense and, rapidly penetrating into the depth of the enemy's disposition, lead the brigade onto the designated axis. And this was at night, on unfamiliar terrain. In sum, we had to resolve an equation with many unknowns. All this in continuing stormy winter weather. The forecasters predicted no quick letup in the storm.

The hands of our watches approached 0200 on 7 January. The brigade commander arrived in the 1st Tank Battalion. He assembled all the officers and conducted a brief meeting. We received the latest intelligence data on the situation. He expressed confidence in the successful accomplishment of our mission in the abnormal weather conditions. And bade me farewell with the words, "I know there will be difficulties. I have faith that you will not be driven off your course. Forward, and only forward! Do not be looking to the flanks!"

The snowstorm howled. We were glad for this. Snow and a cold, gusty wind drove the Germans into their shelters and deep dugouts. The Emchas, painted white, blended into the white background and were hardly distinguishable in the gusty snowy swirls.

At 0300, Nikolay Mikhno issued the detachment the order, "200" (commence the attack). With muffled engines, the tanks moved to the forward edge. The sappers guided us through the passage lanes in our own minefields. They directed us precisely through the narrow lane prepared in the enemy's explosive obstacle belt. Our artillery was silent, prepared at any moment (upon signal) to open fire. Because of the weather conditions, the use of close air support was totally out of the question. We were counting on surprise.

The column of the forward detachment crushed the enemy in his first position on a narrow sector of the front. The brigade's main body crashed into the enemy's position behind us while still in march formation. The distance between tanks was twenty to twenty-five meters. In such a column formation, each Sherman could fire only in one direction, with hardly a deflection to the left or right. Only the lead tank had a full sector of frontal fire. The Emchas' machine-gun fire was supplemented by submachine-gun bursts from the *tankodesantniki*. When necessary, the motorized riflemen also hurled their grenades.

The detachment's stunning strike, and that of the brigade main body, in the middle of the night, in such crazy weather, turned out to be a complete surprise to the enemy. There was practically no resistance along the forward edge and in the near depth of the defenses. Our attack had begun well! Now the main thing was not to be delayed, to break rapidly toward the subsequent nodes of resistance. The detachment hurried: "Speed, speed!" We had to take maximum advantage of the surprise of our attack and the bad weather. And, of course, maintain the correct heading. There were three navigational instruments in the detachment. This was ordered by Lieutenant Colonel Mikhno. I and two additional tank commanders (at the head and rear of the column) followed the azimuth. Such duplication was necessary not only for control but also in the event one of the vehicles that had a gyrocompass broke down.

The snowfall stopped. How fortunate that the weather change found us in the depth of the defense and not at the forward edge. Here the density of enemy forces and means was less. I stared into the darkness. Ahead, slightly to the right, I saw a light. And then the muzzle flash of a shot. I reported this by radio to the brigade commander. His precise instruction was, "Attack from the march! Do not permit the enemy to come to his senses!" Since all the radios in all the Emchas were operating on a single frequency, each platoon and tank commander heard the brigade commander's order. I did not have to repeat it.

We were headed for an important objective of the defenders. The light there had gone out. But we knew the direction to it. The tracks of the lead Shermans threw up whitish vortexes. The light flakes of the just fallen snow covered the vision blocks and gunsights with a thick shroud. We had to clean them frequently.

We came upon a brick factory, the location of an enemy artillery firing position. The appearance of Russian tanks was like a bolt out of the blue. It was our last easy victory. Having worked over the Germans with main guns and machine guns (the *tanko-*

desantniki helped), the forward detachment surged forward. The brigade's main body was behind us about one and one-half kilometers, attacking on our heels. So far, the detachment had not managed to break away from them. Again I demanded, "Increase speed!" The diesels were working at full throttle.

Artillery struck from the direction of the village of Bela. Several illumination rounds burst over our heads. And immediately fountains of earth, mixed with snow, landed in front of the Shermans. The enemy was laying down barrier fires in an effort to intersect our path of subsequent movement. To attack straight into artillery is to swim against the tide. It would lead to unjustified losses. I made the decision to go around the brick factory from the southeast and come in on the enemy guns in Bela from the flank. The enemy had managed to force us off our azimuth. Anything can happen in battle!

Maneuvering along a snow-covered field and opening in the woods, the Shermans came out somewhat south of Bela. The strong gusts of wind were insufficient to cover the noise of our engines. And this permitted the Germans to determine our approximate location. They quickly calculated our coordinates precisely. True, the white paint of the tanks essentially concealed them on the snow-covered field. At high points under enemy observation, our tanks left clearly visible tracks. With each minute, the enemy fire strengthened. One of the Shermans, which had stumbled upon some invisible obstacle, stopped. It was immediately enveloped by thick black smoke. The gusts of wind blew the smoke in various directions, at times clearing it from the engine compartment. New clouds of smoke billowed from the vehicle.

Immense fountains of explosions cut up the field to the left and right of us. The enemy was firing with heavy guns. The salvation of the tanks was in the most rapid closing with the enemy and in increasing the interval between the attacking vehicles. I ordered: "Increase speed! Disperse!" Motors roared. Finally, we drove out of the illuminated zone. Darkness swallowed the Emchas. We left the subsequent series of enemy shell explosions behind us. The Shermans were scattered along a snow-covered steppe. They surged forward. Dismounted submachine gunners ran bent over behind the tanks. Nearby shell explosions sent them sprawling flat in the snow. They immediately jumped up and chased after the still moving "Americans."

The crews conducted volley fire from the march. Even if its effects at night were lower than in the day, it constrained the actions of the artillery crews. It affected them psychologically. We approached the enemy artillery position. The tank of Guards Senior Lieutenant Kibarev was set afire by a direct hit. Driven by the wind, the flames blazed behind the turret, near the auxiliary fuel drums. They should have been dropped off before the attack. But we were breaking into the enemy's rear. It was difficult to foresee how the situation would develop. Therefore, we were forced to ignore the strict requirements of the regulations. Risking his life, the loader, Mikhail Parfenov, climbed out of the tank and put out the fire with a piece of tarpaulin, burning his hands in the process. The gun commander, Guards Sergeant Nasibulin, continued to fire the main gun at the enemy, with the tank commander acting as his loader.

In the end, the Shermans finished off the enemy with their tracks. In an instant, everyone and everything in the position was crushed or flattened. The tanks stopped on my command. Motors were turned off. We needed a breather, and so did our diesels. Most important, we had to set the necessary azimuth for our subsequent movement to Muzhla.

The remaining units of the 1st Battalion arrived. I reported the results of the battle and our losses to Ivan Yakushkin.

Again we set off into the night. We carefully followed our gyrocompass. The detachment captured the Muzhla railroad station practically without a fight. At this time we received a reconnaissance report that Kebel'kut (three kilometers northwest of the station) was defended by infantry, reinforced by tanks, self-propelled guns, and antitank guns. The enemy had managed to activate his closest reserves. Now, we would have to take each village by storm. The brigade commander ordered the forward detachment to go all the way to Kebel'kut, pin down its garrison with fire, then await the approach of the brigade main body.

We fought an intense battle all night for this enemy defensive strongpoint. And by morning it was in our hands. A direct road to Komárno was opened. But I had to go in the opposite direction. I received a new mission from Guards Lieutenant Colonel Mikhno: to take two tanks (with *tankodesantniki* on board) and return along the route we had just fought to Salka, where our night raid had begun, and there pick up fuel and ammunition trucks and escort them to the Komárno area. We wished our comrades success in battle. We would be back soon!

Ice Captive

This story is absolutely true. It is not something from a hunter's fable. I swear by everything that is holy on this planet. In war, as in life, anything can happen.

It was January 1945. Soviet forces were engaged in round-the-clock fighting in the Hungarian capital. On the western approaches to the city, the enemy had launched three consecutive attempts to break through the encirclement of his forces in Budapest. The third, and last (18 to 26 January), enemy counterattack was particularly strong. His intent was to penetrate the Soviet defenses between Velence and Balaton lakes, reach the Danube River north of Dunafoldvar, and thus divide the forces of the Third Ukrainian *Front* into two parts. Immediately thereafter, now protected from the south, the enemy intended to develop the offensive with his main forces between Lake Velence and the Danube toward Budapest, to free his encircled grouping there. This attack would also destroy the 46th and 4th Guards Armies of the Third Ukrainian *Front*. The enemy planned a supporting attack at Bicske [west of Budapest].

In the period from 12 to 17 January, the German command managed covertly to concentrate the entire Fourth ss Panzer Corps in the area southwest of Szekesfehervar: more than six hundred tanks and assault guns and more than twelve hundred artillery pieces and mortars, all on a frontage of thirty-five kilometers. He achieved densities of up to thirty tanks and assault guns and up to fifty guns and mortars per kilometer of front in the breakthrough sector (eighteen kilometers wide).

On 18 January, after a thirty-minute artillery preparation, the enemy launched a powerful offensive. Over the course of three days of attacking, his panzer units advanced to a depth of sixteen to thirty kilometers.

Along the forward edge, in the tactical and operational depth of the defense, Soviet forces undertook extreme measures to strengthen their occupied lines and positions. This was especially true in the corridor between Lake Velence and the Danube. By 21 January, the situation in this area had become exceptionally acute. Enemy panzer formations were breaking through toward the Danube and reaching the rear of the defending forces. An avalanche of supply wagons surged toward river crossings that remained near Dunafoldvar, Baja, and Chepel. Several thousand wagons and trucks accumulated near each of these crossing sites.[1]

After the offensive from the line of the Gron River to Komárno, the 9th Guards Mechanized Corps was in the second echelon of the 6th Guards Tank Army. Its mechanized brigades had suffered significant equipment and personnel losses (approximately 30 to 40 percent). The 46th Guards Tank Brigade (at 50 percent strength) was put on alert on 21 January and sent to the area of Natashstselek, Tekel, and Sigetsentmiklosh [directly south of Budapest], with the mission subsequently to occupy a hasty defense on the threatened axis, to prevent the enemy from forcing the Danube River along a line east of Erd and Erchi. This sector was fifteen kilometers wide. By this maneuver, the Soviet command gave some "insurance" to the forces that were defending on the opposite [eastern] bank of the river.

Brigade units deployed along the east bank of the Danube on the first night in the area of Khalastelek. The town of Erd was in front of us, across the river. West and southwest of this town we could see continuous muzzle flashes of artillery and tank cannons, fires in the built-up areas, and the billowing smoky fires of tanks and assault guns that had been set ablaze. Logistic units continued their frantic rush to the eastern bank of the river.

The order came down around dawn: the 1st Tank Battalion is to move out to Tekel. I led eleven Shermans to the designated area. For us Russians, the temperatures in Hungary at the end of January were not so cold. At night, the mercury dropped to 8 to 10° Celsius. As a rule, during movement at night, each tank commander sat on the left fender of the Emcha and, along with his driver-mechanic, observed the road. They navigated the tank together. This was our habit. At any moment, the existing road conditions could offer up a surprise, frequently an unpleasant one.

On 22 January, we were sitting in a grove of trees along the highway west of the main highway. We were keeping the river under constant surveillance. The situation between Lake Velence and the Danube was changing with each hour. Without consideration for his losses, the enemy, though slowly, was inexorably advancing toward Budapest. Four days in a row the defending units had fought fierce battles with the advancing Germans. The 46th Brigade was dispatched from one sector to another almost every night, first to the north, then to the south.

On 26 January, advance units of the attacking enemy reached the line of the Valivits Canal, ten kilometers north of Lake Velence. Only twenty-five kilometers remained to Budapest. This time, the order returned the brigade to the Danube bank east of Erd. During night marches, two members of the crew, the tank commander and the driver-mechanic, received extra rations. They attempted to bolster themselves as often as possible with Hungarian sausage and even to "warm" themselves. Each Sherman was equipped with two five-gallon containers with a fairly broad, well-secured lid [the so-called jerry can]. A hand with a mug easily passed through the mouth of this container. Inside the container was the untouchable supply of white wine. One had to obtain permission for the smallest dispensing of this liquid. A single dose was three hundred grams for each crew member, but the commander and driver-mechanic were entitled to twice, and sometimes three times, the normal ration. It depended on the duration of the march.

During the course of the movement, especially at night, the driver-mechanic's hatch was always open. Two powerful ventilation fans that drew warm air away from the motors were located under the radiators in the engine compartment of the Sherman. These fans created a relatively strong draft. The wind was cold blowing off the Danube. The commander and driver grew cold quicker and to a greater degree than the other crew members. For this reason, they dipped from the container more frequently and treated themselves to the wine.

A most intense tank-artillery duel was developing on the right [west] bank of the Danube, some five to eight kilometers west of us. We understood that we *Emchisti* might have to fight in just a few hours. Once again, I ordered the crews to check their weapons and ammunition. Our almost daily excursions along the winter roads could have had a telling effect on the mechanisms of our main guns and machine guns. Fortunately, everything was in full working order. Then, by chance, something unanticipated was discovered on the battalion chief of staff's tank. His turret would not traverse, either by electrical or mechanical power.

The chief of armaments, Guards Senior Lieutenant Ivan Korchak, along with the brigade armorers, began to search for the cause of the problem. They disassembled the manual traversing mechanism but found nothing amiss. They reassembled it and tried to traverse the turret again. It would not move. They got involved in checking the electrical mechanism and began checking the circuitry. At that moment, raucous laughter came from outside the Sherman. Guards Senior Sergeant Grigoriy Nesterov was holding his stomach. He was gasping for breath and shouting: "Stop! I have found the cause of the turret malfunction!"

Everyone froze in anticipation but did not expect what they heard next. It was our worst nightmare.

As is well known, whether one drinks a little or drinks a lot, eventually he has to relieve himself. How did we do this on the march? We couldn't stop the column. The tankers managed to "sprinkle" the road on the move, standing in the turret. But their aim was not always true. Some amount of liquid fell on the armor and dribbled down below, to the turret ring. The Sherman's turret was surrounded by protective sheet metal that prevented shell fragments and bullets from penetrating into the gap between the turret and the hull. The tankers' dribbles accumulated in this area. And the ice made its presence known after the cold air froze the liquid.

All the Emchas were inspected. The same "surprise" was found on two others. What if we had entered combat without discovering this problem? Three tanks would have been semioperable. Our joy was not great. I was sure that they would not pat the battalion commander on the back. It was relatively simple to correct the problem. A blowtorch melted the ice, and we wiped away the moisture with rags. The electrical and mechanical mechanisms rotated the turret with the requisite speed. The quick-witted (we had our comedians both in the battalion and in the brigade) could not let such an unusual incident pass without a verse: "*Kaplya za kapley kopilas mocha. L'dom zakovalo bashnyu Emcha.*" [Drop after drop of piss accumulated. It froze the Emcha's turret in ice.]

Others voiced a different sentiment about this phenomenon: *"Supermoshnaya rusichmocha—l'dom polonila bashnyu Emcha."* [Superpowerful Russian piss held fast the turret of an Emcha.]

By the close of 26 January, the German offensive had spent itself. Their stated mission—to break the encirclement of their forces in Budapest—remained unaccomplished, despite the heavy losses they had suffered.

On the morning of 27 January, the Soviet forces launched a counteroffensive. Units of the 9th Guards Mechanized Corps received the order "Stand down!" An assembly area was designated east of the Hungarian capital. We began to prepare for new battles and engagements.

The Charmed Sherman

In war, something often occurs when something else was intended. And it is most upsetting when it was caused begrudgingly or by personal carelessness and inattentiveness. The guilty party in this story turned out to be a nobody, one of the youngest technical personnel, who incorrectly recorded the six-place [serial] number of an Emcha that had been destroyed by fire. He didn't look closely at the last digit and confused "3" and "8." Using this incorrect information, a document was assembled in December 1944 in the 1st Battalion of the 46th Tank Brigade that removed from our equipment list a "live" tank (with the last digit "3") and continued to account for a tank (with the last digit "8") that had been lost in combat near Nadorosi on the approaches to the town of Šahy [north of Budapest, near the Czech border].

Initially, there were no special concerns about this error. I (the commander), my staff, and the deputy for maintenance were aware of the mistake. We all counted on the fact that in an upcoming battle, an enemy round would write off the already written-off Emcha. The more so since the intensity of the engagements with the enemy on the approaches to Budapest was growing with each passing day. As it turned out, however, the twists and turns of combat didn't take our calculations into consideration.

During our maneuvering on the east bank of the Danube River in January 1945, this already veteran Sherman exceeded its maximum engine hours. It was time to retire the tank.[1] But the deputy brigade commander for maintenance, Guards Major Grigoriy Makarenko, was opposed to this action. Our units, as has already been noted, were down below 50 percent strength. Each tank was worth its weight in gold.

Preparations were under way for the Vienna offensive operation. The brigade was supplied with new Shermans. The 1st Battalion had fifteen tanks with "fresh legs," five with average engine hours, and one with "one foot in the grave." The latter brought me—the commander—more than a little trouble and scolding from my superior. On 17 March, the brigade received the order to march as part of the corps and concentrate on the western outskirts of Budapest. The assembly area was about forty kilometers distant. On this modest leg of the route, the "grandfather" Emcha of Guards Junior Lieutenant Viktor Akulov broke down twice. The first time, he had a large oil leak. Then something broke in the cooling system. Simply stated, the tank was straining, it was leaking, it was breaking, and the motors had begun to knock. The battalion had long since arrived at the assembly area, and the invalid was still limping along. I had to listen to an unbearable ass-chewing from the brigade commander. And a stern warning: this would not be tolerated in the future. "The road march was insignificant in length, and yet your battalion is already crippled." It was a bitter reality.

We took urgent steps to repair the invalid. We did everything we could. We replaced the hoses in the cooling and oiling systems, we adjusted and tinkered with various aspects of the engines. Just the same, we were not entirely confident that the repairs we made would prevent future unpleasantness.

On 17 March, we had to make another fifty-kilometer road march. Army units were being moved closer to the forward edge. Akulov fell behind once again. The mechanics and crew quickly corrected the deficiency, and the vehicle arrived at the designated area somewhat late.

Honestly speaking, this unreliable Emcha became a real thorn in my side. It constantly distracted me from resolving important issues of organizing battle in the complicated mountain-forest terrain north of the Lake Balaton area. It threw a shadow over the generally good combat history of the 1st Battalion, of which the enlisted men of the unit were justifiably proud.

That evening, I summoned Viktor Akulov. I looked him straight in the eye and gave him a direct order: "You do everything possible to ensure that this unlucky Sherman burns up in the next fight. Just be sure to save your crew!"

This was the first time I had ever issued such a terrible instruction in all my time at the front. But I didn't see any other way out. We felt that within the next day or two we would be in some fierce encounter with the enemy. Breaking his resistance, our tanks would begin to exploit success into the depth of his defenses, gradually increasing the tempo of the advance. Akulov's tank was clearly not capable of such activity.

On 19 March, the 6th Guards Tank Army was committed to battle. In coordination with other armies, it was to destroy an enemy tank grouping between Lakes Velence and Balaton.

By midday, units of the 9th Guards Mechanized Corps were approaching Bodajk (a village just south of Mor, sixty kilometers southwest of Budapest), an important center of enemy resistance on the approaches to the Bakon hills. A fierce battle was immediately enjoined.

Akulov drove his Sherman to the edge of a small roadside gravel spot. He remained there for several minutes. He began to inspect the terrain ahead with his binoculars. The houses of Bodajk could be seen across the Mor River. The bridge across this water obstacle was intact. Perhaps the enemy had prepared it for demolition. We had to believe that it would be blown up at the first threat of capture by our advancing forces. The battalion's remaining tanks dispersed to the left. They fired a two-round salvo from their main guns. Artillery covered the enemy positions along the Mor River with explosions. The signal was given to attack.

The tanks surged forward. *Desantniki* were hanging on to the grillwork of the engine compartment. I ordered their commander to keep his men on the tanks until I instructed them to dismount. Tanks without infantry in a built-up area, as is well known, can be easily destroyed by enemy tank killers.

Unsuppressed German antitank guns were firing at the attacking tanks. The Emcha of Junior Lieutenant Sergey Lodkov was hit. His crew continued to fire from where they were stopped.

Akulov directed his own tank straight toward the bridge, into the most dangerous sector of the defense. He understood that the crossing site, without doubt, would be heavily covered by fires. His driver-mechanic, Guards Senior Sergeant Aleksandr Klyuev, skillfully using the terrain, quickly reduced the distance to the river. Attracted by the onrushing attack of Akulov's vehicle, the Shermans of Guards Junior Lieutenants Vladimir Yurchenko and Nikolay Kudryashov surged forward behind it. Two enemy antitank guns hurled shells at the brave trio. A solid shot round struck the turret of Akulov's Emcha. It cut through some of the armor, and shell fragments wounded one of the *desantniki*. Yurchenko's tank, leaving behind a broken left track, pivoted around. Two smoke pots immediately flew from the turret, blinding the enemy. They saved the immobile Emcha from a certain death.

The closer we got to Bodajk, the more dense became the enemy fires of all types. Our progress slowed. The *desantniki* dismounted and approached the river under cover of the tanks. The battle moved forward meter by meter, but the attack was threatened. We could do nothing else. It became clear that a frontal attack on Bodajk would not bring success. The corps commander, General Mikhail Volkov, ordered the 46th Tank Brigade to consolidate at the positions gained. The main weight of the battle for this strong enemy center of resistance lay on the 30th Guards Mechanized Brigade, which was operating to the right of the tankers.

By the evening of 19 March, the bypassing maneuver of the mechanized brigade's units and the frontal attacks of Lieutenant Colonel Mikhno's Emchas took Bodajk.

And so the agreement regarding Akulov's tank was not implemented in the battle that had just been fought. Despite the dense enemy fire, the skilled driver had managed to hide his Sherman in a low spot on the ground. There was a single mark on the turret.

On 20 March units of the 46th Brigade continued slowly to develop success in the western direction—toward Balinka, along the left bank of the Maya River. We were pushing deeper into the Bakon hills, whose heights ranged from 470 to 575 meters. This was uncomfortable terrain for attacking tanks. The roads were in poor condition. There were no places to maneuver around enemy strongpoints. We had to gnaw our way through the enemy defense, expending large quantities of ammunition. Akulov's tank sped through a minefield. An explosion blew off a track and damaged one of the bogie wheels. The brigade's mechanics spent an hour repairing the tank. It was here at Balinka that the thought entered my mind: was this Sherman of Akulov's a charmed tank? After two days of heavy fighting, it was still intact.

Understanding the futility of employing tanks in this hilly region, the corps commander placed the 46th Brigade in the second echelon. All day on 21 March, our brigade moved forward behind the 18th Guards Mechanized Brigade, which was advancing on Tesh (seventeen kilometers southwest of Bodajk).

Guards Lieutenant Colonel Mikhno gave instructions to maintain all fuel and ammunition supplies at 100 percent on all tanks. The corps commander alerted the brigade to be prepared to maneuver to the south. I ordered the battalion maintenance officer, Guards Captain Aleksandr Dubitskiy, to keep a brigade repair team available for Akulov's Sherman. It could not fall behind during the upcoming movement.

At night on 22 March, the brigade received the order to move to the area of Inota (eighteen kilometers west of Szekesfehervar) and from there be prepared by morning for action in the direction of Khaymashker and Veszprém. At dawn, the units began an attack to the southwest, moving along the highway leading from Varpalota to Veszprém. The 1st Tank Battalion was leading. Our reconnaissance detachment was two Shermans from Lieutenant Sergey Krikun's platoon, along with Akulov. Three kilometers north of Eshkyu, a Tiger fired on the *gvardeytsy* [guards men] from ambush. An enemy round struck Akulov's Emcha. It began to emit smoke. The commander ordered his crew to abandon the vehicle.

The first obligation of every tanker, no matter what the cost, is to save his "iron horse"—to put out the fire with an on-board fire extinguisher, sand, or dirt. This time, the *inomarochniki* broke this rule. They withdrew some fifty meters and lay down, keeping their eyes glued on the abandoned Sherman. Several tense moments passed. The "enchanted tank" stopped smoking. At this time, Krikun's tanks were maneuvering to the left, in an effort to reach the flank of the Tiger.

In the situation that developed, the crew certainly should have returned to the Sherman. But Akulov made a different decision. He ordered his driver-mechanic, Senior Sergeant Klyuev, to go to the tank and drive it to cover. Aleksandr quickly crawled to the Emcha and jumped inside. He started up one engine and began to move it in reverse. The Tiger fired again at the Sherman, and the tank burst into flames. The fire grew with each second. Klyuev could not be seen. Two *Emchisti* rushed to the aid of their comrade. They ran up to the burning vehicle, where they spotted Sasha crawling out from under the tank. The left shoulder of his coveralls was bloody. They grabbed their comrade and made a headlong retreat. The fire engulfed the Sherman's engine compartment, then spread to the turret. This time there was no doubt—the "transoceanic" was lost. It was stricken from the property books a second, final, time. It was a pity that one outstanding tanker—Aleksandr Klyuev—was also lost.

A Brief Fight

Of all the tank battles in which I participated, the briefest one occurred in March 1945, near Veszprém [ten kilometers west of the north end of Lake Balaton], in Hungary. And with exceptional results.

The Vienna offensive operation began on 16 March.[1] Three days later, the 6th Guards Tank Army was committed to the battle. Its mission was, in conjunction with other major commands of the Third Ukrainian *Front*, to attack on the Eshkyu-Veszprém axis to encircle the main forces of the German 6th ss Panzer Army in the area of Lake Balaton and simultaneously to develop the attack on the internal front of the encirclement, thus preventing the counterattack of the enemy's reserves from Bia toward Lake Balaton.

The task of immediate encirclement and defeat of the enemy tank group was assigned to the 5th Guards Tank Corps. Its attack on the axis of Berkhida [several kilometers north of the north end of Lake Balaton] was to lead to the encirclement of the enemy in the Sekeshfekhervar area [northeast of Lake Balaton]. On the external front of the encirclement, the 9th Guards Mechanized Corps was launching an attack on the Zirez axis.

During the course of 19–20 and particularly on 21 March, major formations of the tank army waged continuous stubborn battles with the enemy. On 22 March, the 9th Combined Arms and 6th Guards Tank Armies began pursuing enemy forces withdrawing toward a defensive line at the Raba River [a tributary of the Danube River that flows northeastward out of southern Austria].

The 46th Guards Tank Brigade, led by the 1st Battalion under my command, hurriedly moved toward Lake Balaton. The battalion was to reach the Veszprém area and prevent the withdrawal of enemy units to the northwest. It was a crucial mission. My force was not great—eighteen Sherman tanks with about fifty *desantniki* on board. The success of the upcoming battle depended much on the rapidity and decisiveness of the actions of each individual tanker in isolation and of the unit as a whole.

The battalion burst into Eshkyu from the march. It destroyed a large part of the garrison with main gun and machine-gun fire and dispersed the remainder. Without a minute of delay, we hurried on. Forward!

By the end of the day on 22 March, the battalion had reached the outskirts of Khaymashker station. The Germans met us on the hills north of this railroad station with strong antitank fire. They set one tank ablaze. More losses were unavoidable. We had to find a way around this enemy pocket of resistance. I looked at the topographical map. Left of the highway was swampy terrain. The Emchas could get bogged down. To the right was a forest. A cart track ran through its green expanse. I made the decision to bypass the enemy on the right, through the forest. I reported my decision to the brigade commander, Guards Lieutenant Colonel Mikhno. "Good luck!" was his response.

I assembled the company commanders—Guards Senior Lieutenants Grigoriy Danil'chenko and Aleksandr Ionov. I explained the new mission to them. Evening arrived. Darkness settled around us. We turned to the right and began to move straight west. Soon we entered the forest. Initially, we followed a break in the forest and later traveled along a narrow, scratched-out road—a trail. It was really suitable only for horse-drawn wagons. Our combat vehicles barely had sufficient clearance; they were pressed in on three sides. Above were thick branches, on the flanks were pine tree trunks, and under the thick crowns of the forest giants it was dark. We had to light up the path with hand-held lights. We did not turn on our headlights so as not to disclose the presence of our column.

Every meter of the path was difficult. The crews and *tanko-desantniki* got out the saws and axes more than once; they trimmed overhanging limbs that blocked our movement and cut down trees to widen the path. The *tankodesantniki* had to provide security. A group of six soldiers moved ahead, and the same number covered our rear. Everyone else was engaged in the essential lumberjack work.

Grigoriy Danil'chenko—his company was leading the column —held a long staff in his hands. It was marked in two places—the height and width of a Sherman. Walking ahead, he quickly determined the dimensions of the road. At the same time, he marked with an ax which branches to trim, which trees to cut down.

The Emchisti and *tankodesantniki* worked all night. By dawn, they had cut a difficult twelve-kilometer path. The battalion came out on the southern edge of the forest at Hill 235.5, just a stone's throw from Khaymashker. The morning fog wrapped the field and the approaches to the station in a dense shroud. This was both good and bad. The enemy did not see us, but we were also unable to detect him at a distance. In an engagement with him, we would fight at close or even point-blank range, and we would use our tracks. It wouldn't be the first time.

Not stopping, the tanks deployed in combat formation and hurried toward the railroad station. The crews of the right-flank Emchas noticed a portion of the body of an enemy self-propelled gun between the trees of a small patch of woods, right of the road. Words of warning of the danger sounded on the radio, along with a description of the target's location. There was no doubt, it was an ambush. The Shermans of Guards Junior Lieutenant Petr Karamyshev and Guards Lieutenant Mikhail Chezhegov opened fire first on the self-propelled gun. The sharp reports of the tank main guns in the morning quiet served as a signal for the remaining combat vehicles. The gun commanders Sergeant Petrosyan and Junior Sergeant Kazakov set ablaze three camouflaged Ferdinands with coordinated fire. We later learned from a captured German tanker that the crews of the self-propelled guns were sleeping. The Russian tanks appeared totally unexpectedly. The German crews were unable to fire a single shot at them.

The alarm was raised at the Khaymashker garrison. Half-dressed Germans ran from the doorways of homes. Some of them rushed toward antitank guns still connected to their prime movers. But it was already too late. The Shermans burst into the streets. Breaking fences, they raced through gardens, destroying enemy equipment with their tracks, shooting German soldiers and officers. A powerful roar rose above the station from cannon shots, the chatter of machine guns and submachine guns, and the whine of tank engines. They say about such attacks that they are similar to a raging tornado. It is practically impossible to withstand such a frenzied onslaught.

One of the first Emchas to reach the houses of Khaymashker was driven by driver-mechanic Guards Junior Sergeant Khailom Bederdinov. He was a man of warriorlike strength and imperturbable nerve. He always conducted himself with composure and calculation in battle. Bederdinov spotted an enemy heavy gun and two cargo trucks in one of the small lanes. Barely hesitating, he veered his tank into the nearest truck and overturned it, rammed the engine compartment of the other, and drove over the gun with his tracks.

Several railroad cars were standing on the tracks ahead. The Shermans of Guards Senior Lieutenant Aleksandr Ionov's company hurried to the grade crossing. The tankers set ablaze four Panthers tied down on flatcars; the submachine gunners captured ten boxcars full of ammunition and, a short distance from the station, a fuel dump. The battle progressed. Guards Lieutenant Ivan Tuzhikov's platoon, sent forward to reconnoiter, reached the approaches to Veszprém. They spotted a large enemy tank column. "Enemy tanks are moving at maximum speed to engage you," the platoon reported to me. We had to get the battalion out of Khaymashker immediately and deploy it south of the station, where we would take up positions to fire on the approaching enemy. I gave the command: "Do not delay! Everyone move to the grade crossing!"

Ionov reported that he was positioned on the main rail line. I ordered him to move an additional kilometer and deploy on the right side of the road. He knew about the approach of the enemy column, as did all the battalion's officers.

By this time, Danil'chenko's company had come up to the southern outskirts of Khaymashker. An enemy motorized column was approaching the station from the west, along a dirt road. A beautiful target! On signal, the eight Shermans of Grigoriy Danil'chenko simultaneously commenced firing their main guns. Precise hits scattered the trucks. The targeted infantry jumped from their carriers and fled in all directions. A hail of bullets rained down on the Germans. Only a few managed to get away.

I ordered Danil'chenko's company to follow me. We rushed across the tracks, through the fork in the road, moved about eight hundred meters forward on the right side of the highway, and deployed in combat formation. Fate smiled on us! We were very fortunate in our selection of position. Our battalion had deployed on an enemy artillery training area. The entire field was dotted with countless positions for guns of various calibers and cover for their prime movers. Later we learned that this training area had a rich history, having served the cannons of various armies. Sometime in the past, someone had carved out a set of positions, dugouts, trenches, and communications paths. We occupied a portion of this complex that suited our needs. It was fortuitous, to say the least.

At this time, the unsuspecting enemy column continued to move along the highway to the north. As before, Lieutenant Tuzhikov's platoon continued to track it vigilantly. The tension grew with each minute. The sun was already coming up over the horizon beyond the forest. Visibility was improving.

From the moment the Shermans occupied their positions until the appearance of the lead German tank seemed like an eternity to us. Finally, we spotted the lead of the enemy column at the turn in the highway. Tanks were moving in close intervals. Very good. In the event of a sudden stop (as would soon occur!), the march formation of the enemy would be compressed.[2] And then the gun commanders of the Emchas could not miss. Meanwhile, our long barrels remained silent. I had given the order not to open fire until my tank fired. On this signal, we would commence firing solid shot first at the Tigers and Panthers.

I anxiously awaited the moment when the entire column was in our field of view. The gun commander of my tank, Guards Senior Sergeant Anatoliy Romashkin, continuously held the lead enemy tank in his sight. The Shermans of Tuzhinkov's platoon diligently held their guns on the trailing German tanks. Fire was distributed on all the tanks in between.

Simultaneous destruction of the lead and trail vehicles of the column would halt the column for several minutes, and this would be sufficient for the outcome of the battle to be decided in our favor. This was my plan. The rapid-firing main gun of the Sherman would not let us down.

"A little bit more, just a few seconds," I told myself. And then all the enemy tanks were clearly visible. I commanded, "Fire!" The air was torn by seventeen shots that were fired as one. The lead machine was set ablaze immediately. The last tank in the column was also frozen in place. Movement stopped. This is what we needed. Having come under sudden massed fire, the Germans began to mill about. Some tankers began to turn their vehicles right on the road to present their thicker frontal armor to our guns. This gained them very little. Their sporadic return shots were drowned out in the din of aimed fire by our battalion's units. The Emchas realized their superiority—fire from a stationary position—in full measure. The highway was ablaze with burning vehicles. Enemy tanks, trucks, and fuel trucks were burning. The sky was obscured by smoke, and the air grew warm.

This unusual battle lasted not more than fifteen minutes. Twenty-one enemy tanks and twelve armored carriers were destroyed. One Sherman was immobilized, but its gun commander, Guards Sergeant Petrosyan, and driver-mechanic, Guards Senior Sergeant Ruzov, survived. They both continued to fire from position, preventing the enemy from attacking the battalion's flank. There was an immutable law at the front: "In the difficult moments of an engagement with an adversary, fight with the courage of two men, or even three!"

The cannonade grew silent. Enemy vehicles smoldered on the road. The Shermans began to move out of their positions. We had to hurry toward Veszprém, to continue to accomplish our assigned mission. Suddenly, a cannon shot sounded from the forest. It struck the left flank vehicle of Guards Senior Lieutenant

Ionov's company in the side and, listing to the right, it stopped. Four crew members were seriously wounded. The enemy had made an almost point-blank shot.

The thickset and sturdy driver-mechanic, Guards Sergeant Ivan Lobanov, raced to the aid of his comrades. He administered first aid to them and pulled them out through the escape hatch. He laid them under the tank. At some point, his glance paused at the edge of a grove of trees. A Ferdinand was slowly crawling along it toward the road, breaking the young shrubbery. Lobanov quickly returned to his tank, loaded the main gun with an anti-tank round, and sat in the gunner's seat. He found the enemy self-propelled gun with the crosshairs of the gunner's sight, laid them below the fuel cell, and then fired. The projectile penetrated the side of the armored vehicle. Its engine compartment spewed flame. One after the other, the Germans began to abandon their vehicle. Lobanov, not wasting valuable seconds, grabbed a submachine gun and jumped from his vehicle. Covered by the hull of the Emcha, the sergeant commenced aimed fire at the enemy. Not one German survived.

How useful to the driver-mechanic in this battle were the skills of handling the tank weapons that he picked up during the brief periods of rest! He studied, he was trained, and he did not lose it on the training range. The effort expended was returned a hundredfold.

Some time later, the battalion's units approached Veszprém. What we saw on the near approaches to the city was utterly amazing. Eight Panthers stood on both sides of the highway in carefully prepared positions. They kept silent, not responding to our fire. Without delay, the Panthers were fired up from close range.

A prisoner captured a short time later recounted that the German soldiers and officers were stunned and overwhelmed after seeing their large tank column turn into an enormous blazing fire in an instant. Therefore, when our units, raising clouds of smoke, approached the well-prepared defensive line at full speed, the Panther crews abandoned their vehicles and, together with the infantry, ran off in panic.

Undefended Veszprém lay before us. But we did not enter the city. Two or three main gun rounds and about a hundred machine-gun cartridges remained on each Sherman. We had expended our entire ammunition supply in twenty-four hours of combat. Our fuel was also running out.

The main body of the 46th Guards Tank Brigade caught up with us about an hour later. Having topped off our fuel tanks and uploaded ammunition, we moved on. We passed to the north of Veszprém. On 23 March, the 22d Guards Tank and 6th Motorized Rifle Brigades of the 5th Guards Tank Corps took this city.

Thirty years later, I was able to visit Lake Balaton and this beautiful Hungarian city. I walked along its narrow, winding, hilly streets. And with my own eyes I was convinced that my decision not to enter the city on that long ago March morning of 1945 was absolutely correct. The battalion was practically without ammunition and had few infantry. In the complex conditions of a large city, the Shermans would have become easy targets for enemy *panzerfausts*.

The archive will eternally preserve documents concerning this brief but conclusive battle: "At Khaymashker station, the tankers captured a railroad train with ammunition, two fuel dumps, an artillery repair shop with fourteen functioning guns, and four Panthers on flatcars.

"The battalion destroyed and set ablaze 29 enemy tanks and self-propelled guns, captured and destroyed 10 trucks, and killed approximately 250 enemy soldiers and officers."[3]

Racing Like a Whirlwind

There frequently comes a time in combat when the leader has to make a reckless decision, to take enormous risk. He operates by the principle of all or nothing. The situation demands it.

After bypassing Veszprém, units of the 46th Brigade fought a several-day battle in the Bakon hills. By nightfall on 26 March 1945, the brigade's tanks had reached the approaches to Tapolca [thirty-five kilometers northwest of Veszprém]. The forested mountains were now behind us, and the northwest Hungarian plain stretched in front of us. Great possibilities were opened for a rapid offensive.

The enemy was making desperate efforts to hold us in the Lake Balaton area as long as possible. This would enable him to conduct an organized withdrawal of his own defeated units beyond the Raba River. The Germans placed significant hopes on this natural defensive line.

The brigade was subjected to intensive air attacks for several consecutive days. Thanks to the presence of large-caliber antiaircraft machine guns on the Shermans, the tankers were successfully fending off these enemy air raids. Elsewhere, another problem turned out to be more serious. In our forces' Vienna offensive operation, the enemy was widely employing mine and explosive obstacles. Over the course of the last two days, four tanks had been blown up by enemy antitank mines. It must be stated that for us, these enemy actions were to some degree unexpected. We had never encountered such a parade of minefields before. Our brigade did not have minesweeping devices to make passage lanes in obstacles. We did not have sappers for each tank. We had to find a way out of this situation. One of my tank officers suggested a possible solution.

The partial platoon (two tanks) of Guards Lieutenant Konstantin Drozdovskiy from the 1st Tank Battalion was out on reconnaissance. This young officer was clever, inventive, and daring.

Drozdovskiy led his Shermans to the western edge of a forest, then stopped. An exposed section of the road led toward Tapolca. Konstantin carefully studied the approaches to this town through his binoculars. It was an important communications hub on the approach to the city of Pápa [several kilometers farther to the northwest]. The enemy would not surrender it without a fight. The platoon commander observed a truck parked in the road two kilometers from where he stood. Germans were quickly running from the truck, carrying something to groups of soldiers out in the plowed field. The soldiers returned to the truck. It was not difficult to conclude that the enemy was hurriedly unloading mines from the truck and constructing a minefield.

Drozdovskiy reported the results of his observations to me without a moment's delay. He concluded his report by saying,

"I am attacking the Germans; I will disrupt their effort!"

Fifteen minutes later, the lead of the battalion reached the reconnaissance Shermans' position. Their crews had succeeded in setting the enemy truck afire before our arrival. The mines remaining aboard had exploded, and all that was left of the truck were bits and pieces of metal on the road. We determined the exact forward edge and approximate width of the antitank mine-field, but the report that the obstacle had been heavily "salted" with bounding and conventional antipersonnel mines was especially unwelcome.[1] This would seriously hamper our mine-clearing efforts.

The tactical situation required the most rapid movement of our tank battalion to the northwest. We lacked the forces to develop passage lanes through the obstacle. The two sappers attached to the battalion had been exhausted by their dangerous work over the past several days and would require significant time to disarm the mines. Consequently, the tanks would be delayed. This was unacceptable. We needed to make maximum use of the approaching night to capture Tapolca and possibly a portion of Pápa.

What a dilemma! And not a simple one either. But a decision had to be made. The enemy had "given us a bloody nose." Time lost to us worked in the enemy's favor.

I racked my brains, and my company commanders pondered. We sought some means of untying this Gordian knot. We could not bypass the obstacle. Frequent rain had turned the plowed field into a morass, and it was impassable. Drozdovskiy turned to me. He had read somewhere how some tankers, racing a T-34 at high speed, had flown through a minefield. Because of the vehicle's high speed, the mines exploded behind it and did not damage the tank.

"This is a tempting idea. But who will be able to accomplish it in practice?" I thought. As if responding to my doubts, Konstantin suggested, "I agree to race like a whirlwind across the enemy obstacle."

There followed several minutes of discussion. All the pros and cons were weighed. And then, "Good luck!"

We quickly prepared the Emcha for sweeping. We removed the auxiliary fuel drums, took the ammunition from under the floor in the combat compartment and put it in the upper storage racks, and placed the main gun and antiaircraft machine gun in travel lock.

Drozdovskiy himself took the driver's seat of the Sherman and dismounted the remainder of his crew. "It was my suggestion, and therefore it is my duty." In the event something occurred, only one would be lost. The exercise began with a seven hundred-meter running start. Revving the Emcha's motors, he raced toward the mined sector of the highway, piled with dirt, rutted and cratered from bombs. After some seconds, there was an explosion, then another, then several more. Geysers of earth and chunks of road surface showered the racing Sherman. By the strained roar of the diesels, we determined that the tank was still running.

Several more explosions, then quiet. Finally, the light breeze carried the yellowish-black smoke away. And we spotted our minesweeper, undamaged. Konstantin was standing on the left fender of the Sherman, wiping his sweaty face. A path had been cleared through the minefield. But I did not hurry to send the remaining tanks through. For full confidence in the safety of the lane, I thought we should widen the path created by Drozdovskiy. I declared to the column, "We need another volunteer!" Several driver-mechanics stepped forward, among them my own, Guards Senior Sergeant Gennadiy Kapranov. I gave him permission to "inspect" the just-created track marks.

In the evening twilight, the battalion negotiated the minefield at low speed along the beaten track and then hurried toward Tapolca.

Deep Raid

The Vienna offensive operation (16 March to 15 April 1945) was a strategic offensive operation of the Third and left wing of the Second Ukrainian *Fronts*. Its purpose was to complete the defeat of the German forces in the western portion of Hungary and the liberation of Vienna, Austria's capital.

The plan devised by *Stavka* was to conduct the main attack

with forces of the right wing of the Third Ukrainian *Front* (4th and 9th Guards Armies) and the supporting attack with forces of the left wing of Second Ukrainian *Front* (46th Army and 2d Guards Mechanized Corps) in the general direction of Vienna.

The shock group of the Third Ukrainian *Front* consisted of 18 rifle divisions, 3,900 guns and mortars, and 197 tanks and self-propelled guns. More than 800 aircraft of the 17th Air Army were in support of this force. The shock group of the Second Ukrainian *Front* consisted of 12 rifle divisions, 2,686 guns and mortars, and 165 tanks and self-propelled guns.

The shock group of the Third Ukrainian *Front* (4th and 9th Guards Armies) launched their offensive on 16 March. Having broken through the enemy's defenses north of Szekesfehervar, this force began to move forward in a western and southwestern direction. The enemy was offering stubborn resistance. On 19 March, the 6th Guards Tank Army, to which my unit belonged, was introduced into the fight.

On 30 March, mobile formations of the right wing of the Third Ukrainian *Front* crossed the Austrian border. Having seized the towns of Sopron and Wiener-Neustadt between 1 and 4 April, the *front's* forces had reached the approaches to Vienna. To crush the enemy's fierce resistance, the Soviet command decided to bypass the city with forces of the Third Ukrainian *Front* from the south and with forces of the Second Ukrainian *Front* from the north. By 11 April, the front line had reached the near approaches to the Austrian capital. Fighting had begun for the city itself.

By the conclusion of 13 April, Vienna had been swept clean of enemy forces.

Tanks are not made for cities! Their combat capabilities are sharply reduced there: maneuverability is limited; engagement ranges are, for the most part, extremely close; without adequate infantry support, these combat vehicles can be relatively easily destroyed by enemy antitank gunners from close ranges and from concealed positions. Tank units strive to bypass cities. There were, however, occasions when the order firmly stated, "Go in!"

Early April 1945. Formations of the 6th Guards Army had seized the cities of Sopron and Sombatkhey in northwest Hungary. Vienna was about sixty kilometers away. We had to interfere with the Germans' efforts to mine and destroy historical monuments and bridges, to move industrial equipment and cultural treasures out of Austria's capital. The army commander, Colonel-General A. G. Kravchenko, made the decision to send a detachment to Vienna. This detachment consisted of the 1st Tank Battalion, 46th Guards Tank Brigade (eighteen Shermans), three SAU-152 guns [Samokhodno-artilleriyskaya ustanovka, self-propelled gun, of 152-mm, or 6-inch, bore diameter], and a company of airborne troops—eighty men from the 1st Airborne Battalion of the 304th Airborne Regiment, commanded by Guards Lieutenant Nikolay Georgievich Petukhov. The detachment was ordered to function as a raiding detachment in the enemy's rear area, hurriedly reach Vienna, penetrate into the city center from the south, and seize key objectives: the parliament building, art history museum, opera house, Belvedere Palace, and Academy of Sciences. We were to hold the captured buildings and surrounding blocks until the arrival of the main body of the 9th Guards Mechanized Corps. The crews were briefed that they would be operating in the enemy's backyard for twenty-four hours, possibly even longer.

The army commander cleverly included in the detachment the high maneuverability and firepower of tanks and self-propelled guns with the practiced ability of airborne troops to fight fierce and prolonged battles in the enemy's rear. It was ever so strictly ordered: "Except in the most extreme case, do not become engaged in combat on the way to the Austrian capital!"

We began our careful preparation for this unusual and, we understood, difficult raid on the evening of 8 April. Two crates of captured chocolate (one could live several days on them) were placed on each Sherman and, more important, the tanks and self-propelled guns were loaded with two norms of ammunition.

The preparations and concerns took two hours. Everything was ready for the departure! The crews and paratroopers slept. How many hours would they have to combat the enemy without sleep or rest? No one knew.

Morning, 9 April. A thick fog blanketed the earth. The infantry at the forward edge did their uneasy work—they penetrated the enemy's defense. We received the signal, "90" ("Tanks, move out!").

As the detachment commander, I shared a single thought and emotion with each tanker—get to Vienna quickly. Two circumstances dictated such operations. First, the objectives designated for capture were located a significant distance from the front line. Their defense might still not be well organized. Second, the Germans were unlikely to conceive of the idea that the Russian command would take this unbelievably risky step—inserting tanks and infantry into such a large metropolitan area.

The battalion column approached the southern outskirts of Vienna, the area of Favoriten. From here lay the shortest path to the center of the Austrian capital. An antitank gun fired from behind an earthen wall dating from the Middle Ages, setting one Emcha ablaze. Our hope for surprise on this axis had vanished. I ordered the unit to withdraw to the northern outskirts of Erla. The crews and paratroopers quickly ate their rations. I called a conference of the company commanders, and we discussed the developing situation. All the officers agreed: execute a maneuver, try our military luck at another spot. This was a normal course of action in such circumstances. But where should we make this effort?

The southeastern sector of Vienna had several less dense built-up areas near the Danube canal. Honestly speaking, however, we did not have full confidence that the approach of Russian tanks to the city was not known here also. That is, on the new axis (if we went that way), we might not be able to achieve the necessary security for movement. One thing was sure. If we continued on our present course, we would suffer more losses.

We studied the layout of the southwestern sector of the Austrian capital. We were looking for a route through Meydling to the city center. There were substantial obstacles—hilly terrain covered by a forest and a winding road. The enemy would not need substantial forces to delay us. We decided upon a variant—bypass Vienna from the southwest and break into the city in the sector of the Hutteldorf-Linz highway.

Austria's main highways were in excellent condition. The fires of war had not yet touched them. They were lined with tall, leafy trees. Their interarching green borders camouflaged the detachment well from the most dangerous threat in this situation—enemy aviation.

Darkness was approaching when the battalion reached the bridge west of Hutteldorf. Barricades blocked the streets and approaches to the bridge. Antitank fire struck the tank of Guards

Senior Lieutenant Grigoriy Danil'chenko, commander of the 1st Tank Company. We were forced to withdraw a bit. We maneuvered to the right and reached Hakking. Our mission was growing more difficult as time passed! Here a solid fortress wall of some length blocked our path. We could not go around it. Time was slipping away. We had to ram it with a tank. Guards Sergeant Nikolay Oseledkin, a driver-mechanic, executed this task masterfully. First he made a small breach. With several strikes of the tank's bow, he enlarged the breach until a Sherman could drive through it. The guards tankers christened this breach the "triumphal arch."

Tanks with paratroopers clinging to them hurried along the railroad embankment toward the western station. The city was going about its normal daily life—buses were plying the streets, trolley cars were clanging, and the Viennese people were scurrying about their business. Traffic policemen signaled our column forward without delay at three intersections. But this atmosphere did not last long. Soon the situation changed radically. They recognized us. One after the other, the canal bridges on our battalion's route of march went up in smoke. There were a lot of them.

Each Emcha commander had a map of the city. This permitted the detachment to continue closing on our designated objectives along multiple routes.

At 2300 on 9 April, I reported to the brigade commander by radio: "We have reached the center of Vienna!" And so the first part of our combat mission was accomplished. The second—no less difficult—was to hold the captured area until the arrival of our own forces.

The principal concern of a commander in such situations is the organization in the briefest time of a defense and, in particular, its most important element—a system of fire. The tankers and paratroopers were arrayed so that each street, intersection, and passageway was under our constant observation. If an enemy appeared, he was destroyed by concentrated fires of all systems. The SAU-152s were our reserve for reinforcing the threatened axis or sector in the course of the battle.

On my order, Guards Lieutenant Nikolay Petukhov's paratroopers carefully began clearing the blocks adjoining the area occupied by our force. Their task was to clean out enemy soldiers. The fact that the electricity remained functioning in central Vienna until 0200 initially facilitated the accomplishment of this mission. As soon as the enemy realized the situation, he turned out the lights.

The night was uneasy. Knowing the city well, the Germans made several reconnaissance forays. They threw grenades at our tanks from the roofs and upper floors of houses. We had to park our Shermans under the archways of buildings. The paratroopers quickly liquidated this danger from above. The crews did not sleep. All were at their battle stations, prepared to defeat an enemy attack. Only near morning did the driver-mechanics and gun commanders manage to snatch a bit of rest. No one doubted that at dawn the enemy would launch his attack. And we were not mistaken. The enemy made his first strong attack in the morning.

Not long before this, the Germans had begun to fire with an antitank gun at an Emcha parked under an arch. During the night, they had dragged it to the upper floor of one of the houses north of Ratush'. The enemy managed to damage the tracks on two tanks. We quickly had to take appropriate measures to prevent the majority of our vehicles east of Ratush', the university, and parliament from being damaged. We wanted to leave them in those positions because from there they could better engage an attacking enemy.

I called the commander of the SAU-152 battery and ordered him immediately to suppress the enemy firing point. The self-propelled gun, sliding along the asphalt on its broad tracks, took a position on one of the streets on the southeastern side of the square.

All of us were curious. We wanted to watch the self-propelled gun blow the German gunners and their cannon to pieces. The tankers and paratroopers poured out into the street and began to wait. Now, recalling those minutes, I cannot excuse myself. As an inexperienced commander, I committed a serious error. At the time, I permitted these spectators to line the street. We paid a high price.

The Viennese lanes that ran in various directions from the central square were not wide. Beautiful houses with venetian blinds on their windows rose up on both sides of these lanes. Each soldier and officer would learn to his misfortune that these windows would end up on the street. The shot of the self-propelled gun's large-caliber cannon roared forth. The air itself shook. One and one-half floors of the house, together with the enemy antitank gun and its crew, crashed to the ground. And in our own position? With a crash, the powerful shock wave of the shot broke the thin window glass in the houses near the self-propelled gun. Heavy shards of glass poured down on the heads of our spectators. The result was lamentable: scores of wounded arms and backs and two broken collarbones. Thankfully, the tankers were wearing their headgear and the paratroopers their helmets. Their heads remained intact. What now! We were fighting our tanks inside a large city for the first time. Bad experience is experience, just the same!

There was no time to moan or complain. Enemy tanks were already moving along several streets toward the university and the parliament. Infantry were attacking behind them, using the tanks for cover. The enemy was beginning an attack on a broad front. Very well, then, the hour had come to cross swords—armor with armor, fire with fire! We had the advantage. The battalion was deployed in combat formation. The Sherman fired more accurately from a stationary position.

A Panther, the thick armor of its turret and hull forming a shield, was leading the attackers on every street. The long-range cannons of the heavy tanks that stopped outside the direct fire range of our Shermans' 76-mm main guns enabled them to strike our combat vehicles from a significant distance. In this unfavorable situation, the Emcha crews, on general command, employed a minor but important deception. They backed their tanks deeper into the archways. They remained ready to reoccupy their position, on command, and spray the enemy with machine-gun fire.

Battles are decided in seconds. The driver-mechanic of Guards Junior Lieutenant Bessol'tsev's tank tarried a bit too long and was unable to reposition his vehicle immediately. This small lapse turned out to be fatal. The Emcha was hit. The commander and assistant driver-mechanic were wounded, but the main gun was undamaged. The crew bandaged themselves and remained at their stations on order of the junior lieutenant. The immobile Sherman was prepared for an unequal duel with an antitank round loaded in the main gun. The radio operator prepared a smoke pot; its dark gray screen at the right moment would effectively conceal the tank's position.

The rapid disappearance of our tanks, it seems, somewhat discouraged the enemy crews. The Panthers stopped. They hesitated, then slowly moved forward. One of the Panthers turned toward Bessol'tsev's tank, in all probability intending quickly to close the range in order to fire the killing shot. The junior lieutenant understood the enemy tank commander's intention. He ordered the radio operator to throw the smoke pot forward. The thick cloud of smoke began to obscure the archway and the street in front of it. Now let the enemy try to find the target.

At this time, assistance sent by the company commander, Guards Senior Lieutenant Ionov, came to Bessol'tsev by the rear courtyards. Knocking down the intervening fence, the Sherman of Lieutenant Abib Bakuridze approached Bessol'tsev's tank from the rear, quickly hooked a tow cable onto it, and towed it to a safe place.

The Panthers did finally reach the line where they could be destroyed by the fire of the Emchas' 76.2-mm guns. The command went out over the radio: "Take your positions!" Ten seconds later, the archways of the houses on the eastern edge of the central square were bristling with the Shermans' long barrels. A cannon duel commenced at close range.

Combat in cities is a great number of violent isolated engagements, in which success depends on the quickness of actions, the coolness of commanders of all ranks, the mastery of each crew member, and the skill of the infantry support troops. Guards Lieutenant Konstantin Drozdovskiy's tank was in a very good position. The archway entrance into the courtyard was ten meters from the corner of the building. Adjoining the house was a small square. Earlier, Konstantin had prepared a good route for maneuver out from under the archway into the square and back. And not in vain.

Up to one and one-half platoons of enemy submachine gunners were advancing on Drozdovskiy's position. Behind them were two Panthers. The forces were unequal. But the Guards *Emchisti* did not flinch. They skillfully engaged in a one-on-one firefight. The lieutenant ordered the full weight of his main gun to rain upon the infantry, who represented a great danger to the tank.

And then immediately to change positions. Volley fire with high-explosive rounds cut through the enemy submachine gunners very well. Those who survived immediately turned back and took cover behind the tank and in a house. The sector of observation and fire was better from the new position. Konstantin saw two armored vehicles approaching the square. They were almost in one line, in places shielding their vehicles behind house walls. There was deep thought shown in this combat formation. The Germans correctly figured that our tank could simultaneously knock out both targets with a single shot. An intact Panther managed to detect and hit an Emcha before the Sherman's crew was able to reload their main gun. In this single action, the enemy tank commanders demonstrated that they were not novices on the battlefield. Drozdovskiy accepted the enemy's challenge and turned out to be more clever than the Germans. The first antitank round struck the right flank Panther on its left track. The intact right track drove this tank to the left, pressing the adjacent tank into a wall. Both enemy tanks froze in place. At the same instant, a smoke pot flew from the turret of Drozdovskiy's tank. The thick cloud of smoke filled the square and street, depriving the Germans of any possibility of conducting aimed fire. Konstantin again changed his position. When the whitish shroud of smoke dissipated somewhat, the guards spotted a backward-moving Panther. A precision-fired antitank round forced it to stop in the middle of the street.

My command observation post was in the opera house. My reserve, the SAU-152 battery, was nearby. Radio reports were coming in from the company commanders. I was monitoring the conversations of platoon leaders with their subordinates, describing the axis of the enemy's main attack from a position north of Ratush' and the university to Belvedere Palace. The enemy's intentions were manifestly obvious: to divide our detachment's combat formation into two parts, press the larger (eastern) portion toward the Danube canal, and destroy it.

As a result of an almost forty-minute fight, the attacking tanks and infantry were halted at the approaches to the central square, three Panthers were destroyed, and we lost two Shermans. Not less than fifty enemy submachine gunners were killed or wounded. Our method of combating tanks—"hunting with Borzois"—that we had tested in past battles was not used in beating off the Germans' attack. Although I reminded everyone about it before the battle, I did not require its employment during our first encounter with the enemy. Drozdovskiy made one unsuccessful attempt, from out of a narrow alley. Not one Panther presented its flank to him, therefore he did not engage them. The damaged track of a heavy tank can be repaired in a short time. Meanwhile, this armored pillbox is capable of conducting powerful fire with its long-range gun. The enemy, gathering up his forces, could once again launch his attack with the support of the immobilized Panther.

I had to turn the developing situation in our favor. And the quicker the better for our subsequent presence in Vienna. Our self-propelled guns were an effective means at my disposal. I discussed a plan of action with Senior Lieutenant Yakov Petrukhin, the battery commander of the big *SAUs*. We agreed on the following: the self-propelled guns, employing the long range and firepower of their 152-mm guns, would strike first at the mobile Panthers. Their second priority was to fire on vehicles that had already been hit. This method would minimize the expenditure of ammunition. We faced many hours of combat before the arrival of our own troops. The battery commander would pay special attention to concealing the movement of his self-propelled guns into firing positions. The Sherman crews would try at this time to distract the attention of the enemy tankers, conducting fire in order to blind them.

Yakov Petrukhin reported that he had selected two very suitable firing positions: they had good cover in front to defend the hull of his vehicles from enemy armor-piercing shells.

The firing intensity increased from our side along the entire eastern line. The *Emchisti* were attempting to solve two problems at once: to prevent the Germans from spilling out onto the central square by blocking them up in the surrounding streets and to cover the movement of the self-propelled guns to firing positions.

How slowly time passes when one awaits the decisive moments in a fight with the enemy. There was no doubt—the turning point was near. The long-awaited time had arrived. Two thundering shots assaulted our eardrums, blowing the glass out of the windows of nearby houses and rattling other windows some distance away. "Pardon us, beautiful city, that we cause you to tremble, and at times, we destroy parts of you! The laws of war are ruthless!" I wanted to cry out loudly, seeing the destruction we were causing.

The second Viennese spectacle turned out to be no less impressive. The strike of a large-caliber projectile (Yakov had ordered a concrete-breaking round loaded, for greater effect) knocked the turret off one of the Panthers that had already almost crawled into the square. The second heavy tank blazed up in an enormous fire. The SAU-152 immediately abandoned its position. It was as if they had poured boiling water on the enemy. The awkward armored vehicles hurriedly began to withdraw rearward. The enemy infantry, now lacking tank support, ran away through courtyards and alleys.

And so the enemy's first attempt to divide the raiding detachment suffered defeat. The Shermans and paratroopers stubbornly held the center of Vienna. I reported the battalion's situation to the brigade commander. He informed me that corps units were conducting a successful attack on the southern approaches to the Austrian capital.

Our chain of command took all necessary measures to provide air cover for the detachment. Thanks to their efforts, the battalion was not once subjected to German air attack during our entire time in the city. On the morning of 10 April, our fighters appeared in the sky above Vienna. We signaled our positions to the pilots with red rockets and sent them a radio password.

An air battle took place a bit later. One after the other, two Messerschmitts went down in flames. Trailing streamers of black smoke, they crashed into a forest. One of our aircraft was also shot down. A small speck separated from it, and several seconds later, the canopy of a parachute opened above it. The pilot was descending into the city. Suddenly, a Messerschmitt dove on him out of the clouds. An instant later, it was going after the defenseless pilot. Two Shermans simultaneously fired their antiaircraft machine guns. The enemy fighter broke off without firing the deadly burst.

The parachutist was well oriented and, controlling his direction of descent with the risers, came down over us. It is quite risky to land in a city. He could land on the roof of a house, strike against a wall, or be hung up in a tree. He had to be extremely attentive. The "sky ghost" failed to see a high-voltage line and caught his risers on its wires.

How could we get him down? It was dangerous for him to jump—the distance to the ground was too great. We stretched a tarpaulin between two Shermans, with the edges tied to the turret hatches. The pilot unbuckled his parachute harness and dropped like a rock. The strong canvas net cushioned the heavy blow. Giving way slightly, the tarpaulin threw the pilot upward. He quickly found himself in the tankers' embrace.

The detachment's personnel had not eaten hot food in more than a day. They were eating dry rations. If my memory serves me correctly, in the center of Vienna was a restaurant that went by the name Astoria. I decided to order dinner for 180 people at this establishment. I delegated the battalion chief of staff, Guards Senior Lieutenant Nikolay Bogdanov (who spoke German fluently) to reach an agreement with the restaurant owner. The desired meal time was 1200 (Moscow time). We had foreign currency—dollars, pounds sterling, and shillings—to pay for the dinner.

There was no doubt that the enemy's morning attempt to attack our positions would not be his last. Taking advantage of the coming lull, I headed for the area of the art history museum with a group of officers. It was possible that the Germans would again throw themselves at us from the Ottakring or Funfhaus sectors. We had to inspect the organization of the defenses on the approach to the museum and make some adjustments to the system of fire based on the experience of the enemy attack we had just defeated. I repositioned the SAU-152 battery to an area south of the parliament.

After conducting the necessary work with the units, I decided to take a quick glance at the museum, to see its displays. We entered the building and were stunned. The halls were completely empty of paintings or sculptures. The walls showed only various sized dark rectangular and oval patches, signs that canvases hung here at one time. During the war years, each of us had seen the fascists' crimes more than once. And here was their latest crime: the theft of the artworks and historical artifacts that were the state property of Austria.

Passing through the labyrinth of large and small halls, we found ourselves in a cellar area. Immense joy flooded over us: here were stacked hundreds of latticed, reinforced crates. As it became clear, these crates contained the museum's displays—

paintings, sculptures, and so on. It was obvious to everyone that the Germans were preparing to ship them. The hurried entrance of our raiding detachment into Vienna had disrupted the enemy's plans. These priceless treasures had not disappeared!

I returned to my command observation post in the left wing of the parliament. Nikolay Bogdanov and the restaurant owner were waiting there. The Austrian wanted to confirm one important detail of the upcoming meal. What kind of alcoholic beverages should be served? I thought about it for several seconds. This was not a minor issue. So I decided to allow the *Emchisti* and the paratroopers to drink a limited amount. They had earned it. "And what does the proprietor of the Astoria have?" I asked Bogdanov. "Cognac." I calculated that the troops had gone more than a day without sleep or rest. How strong a potion would not harm our mission? "And what else does he have, besides cognac?" "French champagne!" The restaurateur raised the thumb of his right hand and pronounced, "Gut!"

Who would have believed it! Where, and when, would we dirty-coveralled tankers get a chance to drink such nectar! I ordered champagne for the tables, one bottle for every two men. "Does the manager have an adequate supply?" I turned to Bogdanov. The Austrian made a mental calculation and replied affirmatively, "Ninety bottles is nothing!" We agreed on this quantity.

Thirty minutes before the appointed meal hour, the restaurant owner invited the battalion command to the covered tables. The table appointments were beyond criticism: snow-white table linens, nickel-plated utensils, and beautiful porcelain ware. In sum, everything was high class. Without a word from us, the owner and the chef walked around all the tables and sampled each prepared dish. This in itself guaranteed the quality of the meal.

The command went out to all the units: leave half the crews and paratroopers in the positions, and the remainder come to the Astoria for dinner! Thirty minutes was allocated for the meal, followed by a changeover of the personnel. Departure from and return to the positions were to be conducted with the strictest observation of security measures.

The tankers, artillerymen, and paratroopers liked dinner. Yes! This was their first such feast along their wartime roads (for some, thousands of kilometers). No doubt, they would remember it for the rest of their lives.

My deputies, chiefs of services, and I (seven persons altogether) began to discuss how much money to pay for this fare and with what currency. I will openly admit that we all were total novices in these matters. We made a "Solomonic" decision, to let the restaurateur himself present us with a bill for the meal and specify the currency of payment.

The battalion chief of finance services placed three stacks of currency on the table: dollars, pounds sterling, and Austrian shillings. We called over the owner of the Astoria. Nikolay Bogdanov explained what was required of him. He hesitated a bit with his answer, and then expressed a preference for "greenbacks." He named a sum. I took the stack of dollars, the bank seal still affixed, and, saying "Bitte!" handed it to the Austrian. With a slight tilt of his head, he accepted the money and immediately secreted it in the inside pocket of his jacket. After several seconds, he pulled the money out of that location and hurriedly thrust it into his pants pocket, not releasing it from his hand. With some trepidation in his eyes, he threw a hurried glance in our direction. The pupils of his eyes (I wasn't the only one who noticed) were greatly enlarged. What was bothering him? Unfortunately, we never found out. My tank commander, Guards Lieutenant Ivan Filin, came running in and exclaimed, "The Germans are attacking again!" We flew out from behind the table like the wind. Everyone hurried to his combat post.

We defeated this German attack, from the Funfhaus area in the direction of the art history museum and the opera house, easily and quickly. Having lost one tank and perhaps thirty soldiers and officers, the enemy withdrew to his starting positions. We had six wounded and two killed.

By the evening of 10 April, attacking units of the 9th Guards Mechanized Corps broke through toward the center of Vienna through Meydling. The Shermans filled the streets and lanes of the Austrian capital. Our raiding detachment had accomplished its difficult combat mission! The battalion had fought in the enemy's rear, separated from the brigade and corps main bodies for twenty-four hours. The enemy had lost four tanks, two anti-tank guns, and approximately one hundred soldiers and officers. Our ranks were also depleted: four Emchas were destroyed, ten men were killed, and fifteen were wounded. In these most difficult conditions, the detachment's soldiers and commanders displayed exceptional endurance, courage, and determination. They had mastered their experience of combat in a large city.

All the enlisted personnel of the 1st Tank Battalion, 46th Guards Brigade, the paratroopers, and the artillerymen were recommended for decorations. Later, I was awarded the esteemed rank of Hero of the Soviet Union.

On 13 April 1945, after stubborn street battles, our forces took full control of the city of Vienna. Many of our troops were awarded the medal "For the Capture of Vienna."

The first anniversary of Victory Day was being celebrated in our unit on 9 May 1946. At a ceremonial dinner on the occasion of this holiday, one of the officers said, "Hey, this is not even half the dinner we had in Vienna!" Those commanders who understood what he was talking about began to laugh. "What did you expect?"

I immediately questioned the chief of finance: "How much did we pay the owner of the Astoria for our meal?" "Comrade commander, do you remember the denomination of the bills in that packet of money?" "I think they were $100 bills." "Yes. And there were fifty of them." "Damn!" "We paid that hospitable Viennese $5,000 for that dinner."

That's what we thought at the time. Sometime not too long ago, I had a conversation with one of our Russian embassy officials. I told him about those long-ago April days of 1945 and about the dinner in Vienna and our settlement with the restaurateur. He corrected me. "There were not fifty, but one hundred $100 bills in that packet. This was the traditional bank packet!" This is why the Austrian's eyes got so big. It turns out that we, simple Russian soldiers, paid him generously! Probably no one had ever settled a bill so lavishly in this restaurant. So much so that it left him speechless.

Give Us Smoke!

After the capture of Vienna, the 46th Guards Tank Brigade units spent several days in the second echelon of the 9th Guards Mechanized Corps. This permitted the crews to get much needed rest, unwind, and take baths. Headquarters at various levels drew up their award recommendations, dispatched the remains of soldiers back to their homeland, and settled monetary accounts. The latter requires some clarification.

On 24 May 1943, the People's Commissariat of Defense published an order, "Concerning the Compensation of Soldiers and Commanders for Combat Destruction of Enemy Tanks." This order established an award of 1,000 rubles for each destroyed tank.

Before the Jassy-Kishinev operation (early August 1944), a gathering of the enlisted personnel in the 233d Tank Brigade resulted in the following decision: from that moment forward, to award the prize money of the "Dnestrovtsy" for destruction of enemy tanks or self-propelled guns to the families of their comrades who had fallen in battle.[1]

For example, the 1st Tank Battalion destroyed thirty-four enemy armored combat vehicles around Veszprém. The battalion's enlisted personnel were entitled to a sum of 34,000 rubles. The approximately 5,000 to 7,000 rubles per company were divided up and given to the families of company soldiers killed in battle. The unified spirit of the Emcha crews maintained this tradition to the last day of the Great Patriotic War.

On 18 April 1945, the brigade was committed to battle and began to exploit successes achieved earlier north of Vienna. By the close of the day, brigade units had reached the town of Pasdorf. The crews refueled and rearmed their tanks, then rested. Early on the morning of the following day, we set out again in the direction of Mistelbach. We moved not more than fifteen hundred meters, then bogged down. Here's why.

The main road passed through an open field about two hundred meters across. On the far end were thick, high bushes. A German Tiger tank, we soon realized, had this opening in its sights. The enemy tank had found an exceptionally good position on high ground on the right side of the road about a kilometer distant. This was outside the effective range of the Sherman's main gun. The Germans were well aware of the tactical and technical characteristics of both our Soviet-produced and Lend-Lease tanks. In addition, the morning sun was behind the Tiger, which greatly assisted its crew in both observing and firing from their tank. At the same time, the sun shone directly in our eyes, interfering with our vision.

As soon as the battalion's lead tank appeared on the open portion of the field, a solid-shot round fired by the Tiger tore through the air. The round struck the Emcha beneath the main gun, leaving a deep scar on the tank. The driver mechanic, Guards Senior Sergeant Nikolay Oselegnin, did not lose his head and raced the tank forward. Several seconds later, a green wall of vegetation hid his vehicle from enemy observation. The tank commander, Mikhail Golubev, inspected the area of his vehicle struck by the enemy round. His main gun had been disabled. The Sherman was now without its primary weapon.

What should I do? To continue to advance would mean suffering unjustified losses. I gave the command to halt. The situation was extremely unfavorable, and time was not on our side. The enemy would not ignore us. We had a clear numerical superiority in tanks. But we could do nothing against this one lone beast. To conduct an assault against his position would result in the certain destruction of several of the battalion's tanks. The terrain between us and the Tiger was almost as flat as a table. The enemy crew could fire on us at their leisure. He had several minutes in which calmly to turn the attacking Emchas into blazing heaps of metal.

We could not maneuver around the enemy tank for several reasons. The river that flowed alongside the road had soft banks. The bridge across it was in the enemy tank's zone of fire. It could block any maneuver we attempted with ease. The river's west bank was higher than the east. Were the battalion across the river, its Shermans would be in plain sight. To execute a deeper bypass would require significant time, which we did not have.

There was one way out—to establish a smoke screen between

us and this enemy tank and, under its cover, rush across the open ground at maximum speed. The mild breeze improved our situation somewhat but would require twice the normal amount of smoke.

We had to conduct this work in a hurry. Ivan Korchak designated four men. While they prepared their smoke pots, dismounted *desantniki* unloaded the headquarters bus. They hand-carried our documents forward to a safe place. The battalion column had to back up. We cleared about two hundred meters of road for dispersing the Shermans and our wheeled transport.

I gave Korchak the command: "Light the smoke pots!" The breeze carried the smoke along into the gaps of the roadside shrubbery. Finally, the required density was achieved. My deputy, Pavel Abramov, raised his arm and sharply dropped it. Move out! Our tanks raced across the road clearing, now enshrouded in smoke. The first headquarters bus crossed in good order. The tank engines revved. With a running start, an Emcha disappeared into the smoke that covered the road. Behind it moved another.

Unable to see their targets, the Tiger crew fired two antitank shells in quick succession. They hurtled through the air with a whistle. Several seconds later, the enemy began firing at the smoke sources. It was now becoming dangerous. They might kill our "smokers" and disperse the smoke pots. The road would be exposed, and our plan would be disrupted.

Fortunately, Korchak and his assistants had deployed the smoke pots not in one but in several locations, creating a rectangular smoke screen. It would not be so easy to shut it down. To do so would have required a massive barrage by at least a battery of artillery.

Powerless to disrupt our movement, the Tiger crew became enraged. They fired high-explosive rounds into the smoke screen, wounding one of our soldiers.

Korchak ordered his team to abandon the danger zone. The five of them quickly moved to my tank. The "smokers" had the appearance of Negroes. They were black from head to toe. Their eyes glittered, and their teeth were white. They had done their job.

We pressed on the accelerator pedals of our Shermans and sped down this unknown highway. Despite the threat of losses, the battalion managed to break through to the north, toward

Mistelbach. True, we had suffered ninety minutes' delay. But we had found our way out of a difficult situation. Again past battles had taught us much. As before, so also this time: *"Vyruchil nas druzhok — pustoy dymok!"* [Our little friend — a puff of smoke — rescued us.]

The advance toward Mistelbach continued into the next day, 19 April. In a tank-to-tank duel with a German Tiger, Loza's tank was struck by a German round, and Loza was seriously wounded in the left knee. Loza was evacuated to a field hospital of the 6th Guards Tank Army, where he remained until the end of June. Meanwhile, the 1st Battalion of the 46th Guards Tank Brigade continued fighting, now commanded by Guards Senior Lieutenant Pavel Abramov. When committed to the Prague operation on 6 May, the 46th Guards Tank Brigade had only thirteen of its authorized forty-two tanks.

The brigade's parent unit, the 9th Guards Mechanized Corps, was committed to the general offensive toward Prague on 6 May. The forces of three Soviet *fronts* converged on the Czechoslovakian capital along separate axes, arriving there at dawn on 9 May. Soviet forces continued to advance west from the city on 10 and 11 May and made contact with General George Patton's Third American Army at several points on that day. On 18 May, the 46th Tank Brigade was concentrated in Milin, a small town about forty-five kilometers south-southwest of Prague. On that day, the brigade received the news that it had received the honorific title "Vienna" and ten days later the Order of Kutuzov, 2d Degree.

When all was said and done, the remaining tanks of the 9th Mechanized Corps, along with their drivers, were transferred to the 2d Guards Mechanized Corps. The 46th Tank Brigade, along with other corps units, was dispatched by train to the Far East.

PART 2

In the Far East

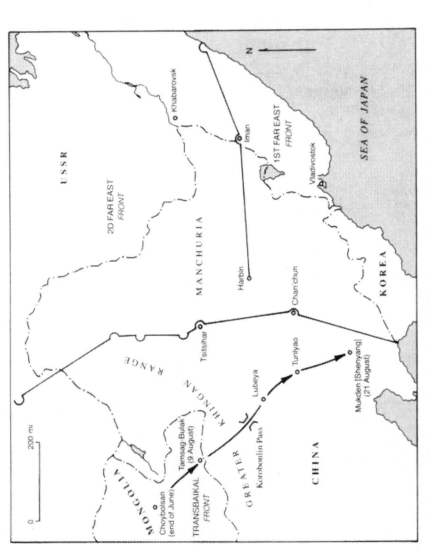

2 Combat path of the 46th Guards Tank Brigade, Manchurian Offensive, June–August 1945.

Greetings, Emcha

The formations of the 6th Guards Tank Army completed their rail journey from Czechoslovakia to Mongolia at the end of June 1945. The 9th Guards Mechanized Corps detrained at Choybolsan station. Its 46th Tank Brigade was concentrated fifteen kilometers northeast of the city. The army's forces had arrived in the Far East without combat vehicles or transport. They were to receive this equipment in their new operational area. Units were at full strength in tank crews, gun and mortar crews, and truck drivers. The headquarters of all troop formations were fully manned with enlisted personnel and had a sufficient number of buses. This permitted them to be included immediately in the enormous effort to prepare the forces for the upcoming combat activities.

The Mongolian steppe was as flat as a tabletop, all the way to the horizon. Abundant rains had recently fallen. The sun's rays had not yet burned the tall green grasses. Everywhere one looked were large herds of sheep. Cattle herders migrated here from the southeastern regions of the country.

For us "Westerners," everything was a marvel: unbearably hot days and somewhat cool nights. We became acquainted with the charms of the sharply continental climate during our first days in Mongolia. Added to this was the absence of roads and clearly visible landmarks.

We lived in tents, buses, and portable accommodations. After two days of this bivouac life, an order was issued: on the morning of 2 July, battalion and company commanders, their deputies, platoon and tank commanders, and driver-mechanics were to be prepared to travel to receive our equipment. The necessary amount of wheeled transport was assigned to the units to move their troops. We would quickly become a full-strength combat unit—a two-battalion tank brigade. Ahead of us were new concerns and great efforts.

It was barely light when the officers and crews were already up

111

and about. Before a tough workday, as before a tough fight, we ate a full breakfast. At the appointed hour, we set off on our journey. The brigade commander, Guards Lieutenant Colonel Nikolay Mikhno, led the column along the virgin land to the south. This greatly surprised us. The city of Choybolsan was off to the right. We always received our tanks at railroad stations. This time, the caravan of trucks was driving away to somewhere in the desolate steppe. What awaited us out here?

The truck column halted after forty minutes of movement. Everyone was ordered to dismount. The brigade commander gave instructions for the trucks to return "home." There was the most complete disbelief on the tankers' faces. Nikolay Mikhaylovich looked at us and smiled. "Why are you depressed, *gvardeytsy*? Now each of us will select an Emcha for himself. His words puzzled us still more. Where in this empty steppe would we find the long-awaited Shermans? After a brief pause, the brigade commander called the battalion and company commanders and their deputies forward. He directed the remaining tankers to remain in place and rest.

Our informal group walked behind Guards Lieutenant Colonel Mikhno. We moved not more than two hundred meters and stopped at the edge of a deep ravine, which stretched out from east to west. We clambered down to its bottom. And it took our breath away. In the sloping sides of the ravine, Shermans were standing every five to seven meters in excavated shelters under tarpaulins. They were hidden from above by camouflage nets. The spectators were stunned. Indeed, what kind of titanic work had been required to drive the tanks from the unloading stations to this place in the steppe; to dig a sufficiently protective shelter for each vehicle; and to camouflage it all so carefully. And this was all accomplished by soldiers and commanders on rear area (quite meager) rations.[1]

The senior lieutenant in charge of the guard force approached us. He greeted the brigade commander like an old friend and then greeted each officer tanker. It turned out that the brigade commander and several of his staff had been here the night before to inspect the "Americans." As we soon learned, all the documents necessary to transfer the equipment had been prepared. "The Shermans await their new owners!" The senior lieutenant laughed. " It appears that our nearly three-month watch will soon be over!" he concluded.

Nikolay Mikhaylovich turned to me. "Loza, pick out your allocated number of Emchas, beginning on either side of the ravine! Shcherban, the rest are yours!" He was the commander of the 2d Battalion.

We quickly staked out twenty-one Shermans. I walked up to the tank designated for me and patted it on the armor: "Greetings, Emcha! Here we meet again!"

Without wasting any valuable time, the company commanders, Guards Senior Lieutenant Grigoriy Danil'chenko and Dmitriy Niyakiy, almost ran back to their subordinates. Soon a cacophony of voices and the clang of opening hatches filled the ravine. The crews got acquainted with their new vehicles. I ordered that a complete and systematic inspection of the Shermans be conducted. I was particularly concerned about the storage batteries. Had they discharged? The Emchas had sat in Mongolia three months, perhaps longer. And when had they left the shops of the American plants? We had no idea. I did not doubt that the batteries of these vehicles that had been idle for so long were Achilles' heels.

Thirty minutes later, I received comforting news. "The primary and auxiliary fuel cells are topped off. The ammunition racks are full!" And a bit later, "The batteries are fully charged!" The heart of every tanker received a joyful jolt: the ringing sound of working diesel motors. My ears had not heard their roar since the nineteenth of April of '45. On that day, I had been seriously wounded near the city Mistelbach in Austria and evacuated to a hospital.

The ground shook from the engines turning over. The torbagany [an unidentifiable species, probably resembling a prairie dog], which stood at attention on the upper slopes of the ravine, timidly scampered away into their burrows. The air turned gray from the diesel fumes. Our hearts beat fast with joy. Our Emchisti took a deep breath of this "sweet perfume." In one hour, we had become "100 percent tankers." Onward!

His Majesty, the Azimuth

The brigade's units were prepared for battle from the moment they received their equipment. The Shermans were fully manned by crews battle-tested in the West. These were soldiers, sergeants, and officers who knew how to "drive with the wind and cut down the enemy with precision fire."

All around us was the vast sea of the steppe, covered with thick grass. There was nothing on it to catch a person's glance. The only salvation in such a boundless landscape was the ability to move on an azimuth. Day and night. For great distances. Without "His Majesty the Azimuth," one could not move a step in these regions! We had some semblance of Western experience in moving by azimuth with the aid of the tank gyrocompass that was mounted on each Sherman. We were required to sharpen our previously acquired skills and adapt them to new and unusual conditions. Crew training was divided into two phases: the first was movement on an azimuth on a "dismounted tank"; the second was practice in this same task but mounted on the vehicles. We planned parallel exercises on the design and function of the gyrocompass and how to use it.

Everything went well as long as the chain of command did not interfere. An order arrived from the tank army headquarters (just as in January '45, during preparation for the attack from the bridgehead on the Gron River): leave gyrocompasses on the battalion, company, and platoon commanders' tanks. Remove the remainder and transfer them to units of the 5th Guards Tank Corps. Twelve wonderful navigational instruments departed the battalion for voluntary service on the T-34s.

A special azimuth drome was prepared on the steppe, with six unequal sides and a perimeter of three kilometers. Half-meter earthen mounds were piled up at the points joining the six sides. On the day of the 1st Company's exercises, for example, the 2d Company sent officers and sergeants out to the mounds.

On subsequent days, the roles were reversed. The task of these monitors was to confirm that the students arrived at the proper point and then hand them the azimuth of subsequent movement with the proper distance to their next point.

On the second day, adjustments were made. The departure line of the designated azimuth route was changed, along with the direction of rotation of the group (if last time we moved clockwise, then on this day we moved counterclockwise). The company commanders sometimes complicated the exercise conditions, adding additional legs. During night training, two or three soldiers with weapons were placed at the earthen mounds. Packs of jackals wandered the steppe.

After a week of intensive training, a battalion committee prepared a new equal-sided polyhedron and tested the units. Thus, we Westerners completed the first phase of our unusual training. The second phase of azimuth training was conducted at battalion level on tanks, by companies. And only in daylight, for quite valid reasons.

July and August are a time of pasturing large horned cattle, horses, and sheep in the northern regions of Mongolia. The merciless summer sun had not yet succeeded in burning the grass here. Several weeks earlier, heavy rains had passed through the area and the steppe was now covered with thick green grass. Even Mongolian old-timers could not recall such rich pastures. This is why the mechanized corps units were close neighbors to thousands of head of pasturing sheep, cattle, and horses. Only small areas of steppe were empty, waiting their hour of grazing. After a short time, the sheep flocks and herds of cattle and horses would wander there.

To conduct night exercises on tanks in these conditions would mean accidentally running over countless innocent animals by tracks. Even in daylight exercises, this happened more than once.

The laws of war are immutable. It comes to mind how, during the preparation for the Jassy-Kishinev operation (August 1944), the Moldavian population was evacuated to a man from a one hundred-kilometer frontal zone to the rear in the beginning of April. At the same time, Soviet Army soldiers continued to cultivate everything that had been planted and sowed in the gardens and fields of the empty villages. Special garden-field teams were formed for this work. At the end of August, the Moldavians returned to their birthplaces and were surprised speechless. A bountiful harvest had grown and remained untouched in their fields and personal plots. All they had to do was gather it in.

In preparing the Khingan-Manchurian operation, our command acted quite differently. The troop deployment areas were not depopulated. Exceptions were made in the great war.

Before their departure to start positions, the Soviet and Mongolian forces were concentrated principally in the northern part of the Mongolian People's Republic. Formations of the 6th Guards Tank Army were positioned west, south, and southeast of the city of Choybolsan, not far from the Kerulen River. In these areas were a small number of nomadic herders with all sorts of herbivorous small and large livestock. The staff officers joked, "There were never such densities of tanks, guns, cattle, sheep, and horses before a single operation in the West!"

We Westerners understood that this Mongolian phenomenon was possible for several reasons. The recent victory over fascist Germany had radically changed the world situation. The fate of Japan—the Third Reich's last ally—had been sealed. The removal of the Mongolian peasant herders from areas of succulent grasses would cause significant damage to the Mongolian civilian economy. The grass in the western and southern areas of the country had all been consumed, and what remained had been dried out by the merciless hot sun.

Thus, we, tankers and herdsmen, lived as good neighbors until the beginning of the August offensive.

Forced March to the Border

The last days of a hot July passed. The *front* chain of command visited the tank army's units and formations regularly to inspect various aspects of their preparation. This was a clear sign that there would be change. In the first days of August, a strict order was received: to turn in all equipment not required for combat to corps and army supply facilities. What was it a sin to hide? We had both captured German automobiles and motorcycles and spare parts for them; the tankers, infantrymen, and artillerymen had a significant quantity of various radio sets.

This "cleansing" of the units continued for almost twenty-four hours. They turned gear in to warehouses, set fire to it, and even buried it in the ground. Then we proceeded to an equally intensive effort: to fill all our personal baggage with water. We loaded each Sherman with two containers of this life-giving liquid. We topped off the primary and auxiliary fuel cells. A complete inspection was conducted on 4 August to confirm the "slimming down" of the companies and battalions and their readiness to execute a movement. By the evening of this day, the 1st Tank Battalion was reinforced by a company of *tankodesantniki*. We distributed them on the basis of five or six men per Emcha. Everything was in full combat readiness. It remained only to press on the starter button and move out!

At the same time, an order arrived on the conduct of a march and the occupation of a start position for the offensive in the area of Tamsag-Bulak. The 9th Guards Mechanized Corps commander, General-Lieutenant Mikhail Volkov, planned for the wheeled vehicles to complete the movement in two legs and the tanks in three.

To avoid overheating the engines of the tracked vehicles, units were to move mainly at night. During the day, the troops rested and conducted maintenance. Formations of the tank army moved on the maximum number of routes. Thus the 9th Corps executed the march in five columns. Corps headquarters sent an operations group ahead to conduct commanders' reconnaissance, trace the march routes, and select areas for the brigade's daily halts. In addition, a movement support detachment was sent out to support the continuous progress of the forces on each march route. Special traffic control posts and light markers were established in sections of difficult terrain to indicate the direction of subsequent movement to crews and drivers that had fallen behind. Markers were placed with coded unit designations at bends and sharp curves on the dirt roads. For example, the recognition marker of the 46th Tank Brigade was the outline of a spade [as on a playing card] with the number "4" inside. This marker was painted on the Shermans' turrets, the body panels of trucks, and the sides of armored transports. Other corps units also had the spade marker but with a different numeral inside.

Each nightly journey was 100 to 110 kilometers long, requiring eight to nine hours of travel. The average movement speed was 18 to 20 kilometers per hour. The Mongolian steppe made its presence known. The extreme dustiness had a telling negative impact on the mechanical condition of the combat and transport vehicles. The movement of even a small vehicle column raised clouds of dense, sandy dust. The Sherman traveling ahead was invisible, creating a constant threat of colliding with it. The intervals between and within units increased involuntarily. But this did not help. Vehicle air cleaners and filters quickly became contaminated, requiring the tank crews and truck drivers to service these components every three to four engine hours. As a rule, this was accomplished on short halts, two times each night.

Significant wear of the suspension components of the Shermans, especially the track shoes and track pins, was observed during the movement in the desert and steppe terrain. Upon arriving at the forward assembly area (having covered a distance of 300–350 kilometers), it turned out that the track pins were worn by as much as 2–3 millimeters and the drive sprocket teeth up to 1–1.5 millimeters. Therefore, a majority of the Emchas required replacement of two or three track shoes.

For brigade and battalion commanders, crews, and engineer-maintenance personnel, the forced march to the border became a sort of dress rehearsal for the upcoming operation. Experience was gained in movement in extremely dusty conditions and in rapidly servicing vehicles at nighttime halts. The chiefs of the engineering-maintenance services came to the conclusion that in the desert and steppe terrain, the Shermans required replacement of track shoes every 300 to 400 kilometers, and complete rebuilding of the track with replacement, for example, of one-third of its track shoes every 500 to 600 kilometers. The necessity of more frequent and careful checks of the lubrication, charging, cooling, and especially air filtration systems was emphasized.

By the morning of 8 August, forces of the 6th Guards Tank Army were occupying their forward assembly areas for the offensive. We did not realize that only twenty-four hours remained until the start of combat activities.

On the Eve

The **Manchurian** strategic offensive operation (8 August to 2 September 1945) was one of the largest operations in the concluding stage of World War II. It is unequaled in a number of operational norms and characteristics. The combat actions were projected to unfold on the broadest scale: troops occupied start positions along a 5,000-kilometer line; the forces of three *fronts* were concentrated in a zone of 280 to 300 kilometers, which made up 7 percent of the front as a whole.

The concept of the conduct of the operation against Japan envisioned forces of the Transbaikal, First, and Second Far East *Fronts* executing a rapid penetration into the heart of Manchuria on three strategic axes. The main attacks were planned to be launched from the territory of the Mongolian People's Republic to the east and from the area of the Soviet Primor'ya [that portion of the USSR bordering Manchuria on the east, basically south of Khabarovsk] to the west. These two meeting attacks were separated (measured along the international boundary) by a distance of not less than twenty-five hundred kilometers. The forces had to capture important military-political and economic objectives in central Manchuria—Mukden, Chan'chun, Harbin, and Gerin—as rapidly as possible. This was to be accomplished by the division of the Kwantung Army's main forces into isolated pieces, with their subsequent encirclement and destruction in northern and central Manchuria. The Transbaikal and First Far East *Fronts* were given a leading role in the operation. Forces of the Second Far East *Front* were launching a supporting attack from the Blagoveshchensk area in the general direction of Harbin. They were to assist in breaking up the enemy grouping and destroying it in detail.

The three *fronts* had a total of eleven combined arms, one tank, and three air armies and an operational group. These formations included eighty divisions (of these, six cavalry, two tank, and two motorized rifle), four tank and mechanized corps, six rifle and thirty separate brigades, and the garrisons of fortified regions [primarily artillery and machine-gun units]. Of the sixty-three tank and mechanized formations deployed in the three *fronts*, twenty-nine—more than 46 percent—were in the Transbaikal *Front*. This was on the axis of the most complex natural conditions, which the Japanese command considered insurmountable and unsuitable for use by large masses of forces and combat equipment.

Altogether, 1,566,725 personnel; 26,137 guns and mortars; 5,556 tanks and *SAUs* [self-propelled guns]; and more than 3,800 combat aircraft were concentrated in the Far Eastern grouping of Soviet forces. The overall superiority over the enemy was 1.2:1 in troops, 4.8:1 in tanks and artillery, and 3.6:1 in aircraft. On the axis of the main attacks, the Soviet command sought to create a decisive superiority in forces and means. Thus, on the Transbaikal *Front*, the correlation of Soviet forces to Japanese forces was 1.7:1 in infantry, 8.6:1 in guns and mortars, and 5:1 in tanks and *SAUs*.[1]

Let's take the Berlin strategic offensive operation (26 April to 8 May 1945) for comparison. It was also conducted by the forces of three *fronts*. Sixteen combined arms and four tank armies, nine tank and mechanized and four cavalry corps, and four air armies were allocated for the breakthrough of the enemy defenses.

Two and a half million men participated in this concluding operation for the defeat of fascist Germany; 41,600 guns and mortars; 6,250 tanks and *SAUs*; 7,650 aircraft, a portion of the forces of Baltic Fleet and Dnieper Flotilla were employed. And all these forces and means were deployed, in contrast to the Manchurian operation, on a continuous front in a zone of not more than three hundred kilometers.

A favorable correlation of forces was created on the Berlin strategic axis. Our forces were 2.5 times greater than the enemy in personnel; 4 times in guns, mortars, tanks, and *SAUs*; and 2.3 times in combat aircraft. The Berlin operation had a modest depth—150 to 160 kilometers.

In the Manchurian operation, the Lend-Lease Sherman tanks operated as part of the Transbaikal *Front*. Therefore, the following material will address the peculiarities of their employment in the complex conditions of the steppe-desert-mountain and inhabited territory beyond the Khingan Mountains.

The Transbaikal *Front* received the mission to conduct the

main attack with forces of three combined arms armies and a tank army in a bypass of the Khalun-Arshan fortified region from the south in the general direction of Chan'chun. The *front's* immediate mission (350 kilometers deep) was to defeat the enemy's opposing forces, overcome the Grand Khingan Range, and reach the Daban'shan-Lubeya-Solun' line with the main body by the fifth day of the operation. The subsequent mission was to seize the Chafyn-Mukden-Chzhantszyakou-Chzhalan'tun' line (800 kilometers deep) with the main body.

The 6th Guards Tank Army received a leading role in the Transbaikal *Front's* operation. Its formations, operating in the general direction of Chan'chun, were ordered to force the Grand Khingan Range by the tenth day of the offensive, reinforce the passes through it, and prevent their occupation by enemy reserves until the arrival of the combined arms armies.

In addition, the *front's* forces were expected to conduct two supporting attacks, on the right and left flanks of the *front*. The zone of the Transbaikal *Front's* offensive along the international boundary was twenty-three hundred kilometers wide, but the active sector, where forces were deployed, was fifteen hundred kilometers wide. The average rate of advance during the accomplishment of the *front's* immediate mission was planned at twenty-three kilometers per day for combined arms armies and approximately seventy kilometers per day for tank armies. The operation was intended to last for ten to twelve days (for tank armies) and ten to fifteen days (for combined arms armies).

Because the Transbaikal *Front* faced weak enemy forces in the border zone, the *front* commander, Marshal of the Soviet Union R. Ya. Malinovskiy, envisioned the employment of the 6th Guards Tank Army in the first echelon with the mission of the most rapid possible capture of passes in the Grand Khingan. For this reason, the combined arms armies were deployed on a broad front and, using strong forward detachments and mobile groups, they were to conduct their offensives on independent axes, maintaining only operational coordination between them.

The surmounting of the Grand Khingan was planned in two phases. In the first phase, lasting two days, the forces of the 6th Guards Tank Army were to destroy enemy border units, negotiate the desert-steppe area, and reach the southern reach of the Great Khingan Range. The depth of this phase was two hundred kilometers, with an average rate of advance of one hundred kilometers per day.

In the second phase, lasting three days, army formations were to capture the passes of the Grand Khingan and reach the central Manchurian plain. The depth of this mission was 250 kilometers, with an average rate of advance of 80 kilometers per day.

The 6th Guards Tank Army's offensive was intended to be conducted on two axes, seventy-five kilometers apart. To reduce the length of its columns, the 9th Guards Mechanized Corps used two march routes during its crossing of the desert, with strong forward detachments and movement support detachments on each axis. The 46th Guards Tank Brigade, to which my battalion belonged, was in the corps forward detachment.

The most unusual feature of the Transbaikal *Front's* Khingan-Mukden operation was that in the course of the offensive, the forces "jumped from the frying pan into the fire," so to speak. They had to cross the white-hot sands and salt marshes of the Gobi Desert, take the southern reach of the severe Grand Khingan Range by storm, and then traverse the swampy fields of the central Manchurian plain. August was a month of monsoon winds, a period of heavy rains.

The *Emchisti* and soldiers with other specialties knew it would not be easy. They were carefully prepared for it, both in matériel and spirit. In reality, every aspect of the offensive turned out to be exceptionally difficult on both the troops and the equipment. On this operational axis, the geographic conditions that included a burning desert, torrents of rain, the dangerous roads and paths of the Great Khingan, and the sticky, loamy soil of Manchuria became, in truth, our enemy number one. How much energy and effort we consumed during this operation is known only to God.

The 46th Guards Tank Brigade occupied its forward assembly area for the offensive on the southeastern slopes of Mount Modon-Obo, fifty kilometers south of Tamsag-Bulak. It was thirty-five kilometers to the border.

Early on the morning of 8 August, the order came down: "Feed your soldiers and rest them until noon. Organize careful security of your units' positions."

Upon receipt of this order, the conjecture that something

big was going to happen made the rounds through the soldiers' own "Informburo."[2] This supposition was confirmed in less than three days.

Intensive work kept the brigade staff busy. In short order, they put together a commanders' reconnaissance plan. The corps command designated one working point for the brigade—Mount Khukh-Ula (in the Barun Ereniy–Nuru range)—1.5 kilometers from the border.

The commanders' reconnaissance group of each tank battalion consisted of four officers: the battalion commander, his chief of staff, and the two company commanders. The tankers arrived at the designated commanders' reconnaissance point at 1800. This time was not chosen by accident. At this moment, the sun was behind the *Emchisti* and therefore did not blind them. The sun's oblique rays illuminated well the close in and far areas of the border region. The group stealthily crawled to the top of Mount Khukh-Ula. They assembled there in a line. In the middle was the acting brigade commander, Guards Lieutenant Colonel Pavel Shul'meyster. On the right were the officers of the 1st and on the left the officers of the 2d Tank Battalions. We were quiet for several minutes, in order to catch our breath from the difficult almost one hundred-meter climb. We were also trying to calm our nerves. This was not a routine commanders' reconnaissance but an important process in anticipation of the war with Japan. It was unique in our wartime experience. Anyone would be subdued in this situation. I had the added responsibility of family now, as well.

Our work began. We took out our binoculars and studied the terrain beyond the border, areas of Inner Mongolia and the Chinese province Lyaonin. We had studied them carefully on the topographic map when we were northeast of Choybolsan. With the occupation of the forward assembly area, the brigade now was tied to a specific operational axis. The goal of this trip to the border was to see this axis with our own eyes.

The experience of countless battles in the West taught us: "Terrain can be your friend or your enemy—study and remember each stream, hill, and gully." They have diverse natures. Some can assist, and some can complicate the accomplishment of the assigned mission.

I glanced over the area immediately beyond the border, a

plain rising toward the southeast. It was covered with short grass, already burned by the sun, and with broad areas of salt marshes and quicksand. This cheerless picture, which stretched out in front of us for sixty kilometers, did not gladden our hearts. Farther out rose the placer of individual hills, that ran from the southwest to the northeast. In the zone of the brigade's upcoming offensive, these hills had elevations not greater than twelve hundred meters above sea level, sufficient to block our view of a significant expanse of terrain behond them. On the far horizon could be seen the southern reaches of the Grand Khingan Range. We Westerners were no longer surprised at the visibility conditions here. The air had low humidity, and its transparency (in dry, calm weather) reached tens of kilometers.

We had to turn to the map. The one hundred-kilometer area around the Khingan was again marshy and sandy. In a word, it would not be an easy road. Not for the tankers, and not for the Emchas. I directed my binoculars once again at the nearby border region. Not a soul anywhere. Two kilometers to the left—*fanzas* [peasant domicile in Korea or Japan] and a Japanese military outpost. There were no signs of the presence of soldiers in it. The Mongolian border troops informed us that on the night of 7– 8 August, all the Japanese departed and headed deep into their own territory. They drove off the flocks of sheep.

Study of the border terrain continued for approximately twenty to twenty-five minutes. The quiet was finally broken by the voice of Guards Lieutenant Colonel Shul'meyster: "Look at the map. Directly in front of us are Hills 1244 and 1268, 'camel humps.' Now, find them on the ground." This required no great effort; they clearly stood out among their neighboring hills.

Lieutenant Colonel Shul'meyster issued the combat order for the offensive on Mount Khukh-Ula. We learned the following from it. The brigade was designated as the corps forward detachment. It was to defeat small enemy covering forces in the border area from the march and maintain the continuous movement of the mechanized corps' main body without its deployment. Hill 1244 was the main reference point for the first phase of our actions. We marked this hill on our maps and entered in our notebooks the azimuth to this "guiding" height. My 1st Tank Battalion was designated to lead the brigade. (I never doubted that this difficult and responsible mission would be given to me and my subordinates.) Guards Senior Lieutenant Mikhail Strugin, formerly the deputy commander, now commanded the 2d Battalion. Naturally, the brigade command wanted a unit whose commander had weathered the winds and storms of many battles at the cutting edge of its formation.

When it reached the northern slopes of Hill 1244, the forward detachment would turn sharply to the south, push quickly into the area of Bayan-Khoshun-Sume, and seize this settlement from the march. Here we would determine the azimuth of the brigade's subsequent movement toward the Grand Khingan Range.

A special order would announce the day and hour of the beginning of the offensive.

Observing strict security measures, as before, we crawled down from Mount Khukh-Ula, assembled in the trucks, and headed for our unit locations. We proceeded quietly. Each battalion and company commander had his own thoughts and concerns. They were many.

The necessary instructions were issued to the battalion staff and units. We stood down immediately after supper. Let the tankers get a good night's sleep. When our adventure began, we might have to go several days straight without sleep. So it was in all the Western operations. The upcoming operation could hardly be any different.

I forced myself to sleep. First one thing concerned me, then another. There would be incredible pressure on the crews. Could they withstand it? I was comforted in the knowledge that almost 80 percent of the *Emchisti* had faced every test against the Germans. They had been washed by rains, tempered by the fires of the Tigers and Panthers. This experience was a guarantor of the success of my subordinates in overcoming the East Asian obstacles. That there would be many (the overwhelming majority of which we had never faced before) we had no doubt.

And the Shermans? They were new vehicles. This made us happy. The August surprises of 1944 involuntarily surfaced in my memory. Romania. The fuel shortage (here we would not find the necessary ingredients to make a tank "cocktail"); the overheating of the track system (in the steppe-desert conditions, we were twice or even three times as likely to become "barefooted"); and the real threat of frequent boiling over of our engine coolant. During the execution of the forced march to the border, we mastered the experience of quickly cleaning the dust from our air filters. We could expect this to be our constant (and hated) companion all the way to the Grand Khingan.

It was by good fortune that the wartime paths of two close relatives crossed at Zima station [in Siberia, 250 kilometers northwest of Irkutsk]. During the movement of forces by railroad from the West to the Far East, several troop trains had accumulated at this station. Near the flatcars and troop cars of our brigade stood the "Pullmans" of some rifle division. From a chance conversation between the soldiers of the two units, it was discovered that my father was among the troops of these "queens of battle."[3] Our joyful meeting ended, using the contemporary jargon, with a "barter deal": we had to give up Guards Sergeant Ivan Savin, cobbler, for Private Fedor Loza, tailor. In the infantry, Savin's specialty was worth its weight in gold. And so, from this moment forward, father and son—private and guards captain—served together.

The defeat of tsarist Russia in the Far East in 1905 caused a special pain for our family. Thirty-year-old Private of the Russian Army Fedor Loza, my grandfather, perished in the first months of the war with Japan in the trenches around Port Arthur. I knew him only from photographs. Forty-plus years later, the son and grandson, along with thousands of Soviet soldiers, prepared to walk on the ground where their forefather rested for eternity.

I put my father, who was engaged in general work and bustled about in preparation for the upcoming offensive, on the back burner. But he wasn't concerned about this, and at times his presence persistently tugged at my heart.

A Leap across the Desert

On the evening of 8 August, we learned that the offensive would begin on the next day. The 46th Guards Tank Brigade was ordered to be prepared for action at 2400. At 0030 on 9 August, the signal was sent out: "Forward!" The roar of the Shermans' diesels split the quiet of a summer night. The brigade's units rushed toward the border.

Phosphorus markers had been placed out on isolated sectors for traffic regulation. Complete radio silence was observed, along with the strictest light discipline. The column moved quickly, observing a fifty-meter interval between vehicles. The tanks' steering controls were in the hands of experienced driver-mechanics. This could not help but gladden a commander's heart.

A bit after 0100, the lead of the brigade march formation reached the western slopes of Mount Khukh-Ula. It was a stone's throw to the border marker. Here we met representatives of the corps staff: operations and intelligence officers. The column stopped. Guards Lieutenant Colonel Pavel Shul'meyster and I, commander of the lead battalion, were informed of the latest intelligence reports. Reconnaissance had gone forward and had not detected any enemy. The corps staff intelligence officer and his radio-telephone operator had been ordered to remain with my battalion. This circumstance greatly pleased us. We would receive firsthand reports on the enemy. One couldn't ask for better!

During our last moments on friendly Mongolian soil, Pavel Shul'meyster shook our hands and wished us success. The battalion set off to accomplish its assigned mission. We quickly crossed the border. I ordered my tank commander to write down the odometer reading. If I—or, if something happened, my replacement—safely reached the final battle position, we would know precisely how many difficult kilometers the *Emchisti* had traversed. This would be helpful for subsequent award recommendations and, later, for history.

Two circumstances—the coolness of the night and the absence

of the enemy—persistently demanded the following nature of our actions. While our troops were fresh, we extracted everything possible from the equipment. Speed, speed, speed. I ordered: "Platoon and tank commanders—on the fenders!" We had done this more than once in the West—at night and in snowstorms. From this moment, three pairs of vigilant eyes would scan the road (more precisely, the terrain): the commander on the tank's left fender, next to him the driver-mechanic, and on the right, the assistant driver-mechanic. With this observation setup and the extended interval between vehicles, we could increase the speed of movement. At this stage of the offensive, this was most important of all.

A second, and no less important, problem was to maintain the specified azimuth. One of the two crews especially prepared to be leading was in Guards Senior Lieutenant Dmitriy Niyakiy's company. The battalion chief of staff and each company commander constantly monitored the correctness of our direction of movement.

We held strictly to a southerly course. We detoured to the west side of an enormous salt marsh, stretching around Lakes Organ-Nur and Bayan-Nur. Our tracks crushed the thick, dry grass, leaving sufficiently deep tracks. Our battalion column's route was well marked by the tracks. It was not hot. Heat later ate up the units coming behind us. We covered eighteen kilometers and arrived at Khitikar-Khuduk well. It was filled with dirt and possibly poisoned. The Japanese border troops, withdrawing into the depth of the territory they occupied, had destroyed all water sources. We did not doubt that we would see similar scenes in other places.

The Sherman engines performed well. The coolant temperature remained "in the green."[1] We altered the axis of the offensive slightly, rushing to the southeast, into the passage between two hills with identical spot elevations—1052. There was a line of a dirt road between them on the map. While the sun had not yet come up, and the scorching heat had not begun, the motto was "don't slow down, tanker, grab the kilometers."

We approached the twin peaks. The plain was covered with withered vegetation. And here nature gave us our first surprise. The Emchas were following one behind the other, in the same track. The first vehicle was moving at a decent speed—approximately thirty miles per hour. The other tanks were keeping up with it. Without any warning, the tracks of the third tank in the column, the Sherman of Guards Lieutenant Mikhail Golubev, began to slip, and then the vehicle quickly settled into the ground. They applied more power. The tracks threw a rooster tail of sand and gravel high into the air behind the tank. We had to stop the column to deal with this developing situation. I walked over to the "captive" tank. It was stuck solid. Without outside help, it could not get out of this trap. I convened a mini-conference: my deputy, the battalion chief of staff, and the company commanders. We analyzed the situation, pondering how best to organize our subsequent movement without reducing speed.

We learned a lesson from this mishap. Under the thin layer of grass was dry sand, fine as ash. The light covering of the desert was capable, in the best circumstance, of supporting the weight of not more than two moving Shermans. Any more caused it to collapse. And so, from this point on, the tanks could not follow in each others' tracks. The battalion had to transition to a double-line formation. The 1st Company deployed on line with increased intervals between vehicles, and the 2d Company followed on line behind it, driving between the existing tracks. If the terrain permitted, we used the wedge formation to the leeward side. This would preserve, to some degree, the integrity of the upper covering of vegetation on the desert. Other brigade units were moving behind us.

During this time, a group under the leadership of the deputy battalion commander for maintenance, Guards Captain Aleksandr Dubitskiy, was developing a method to recover Mikhail Golubev's mired Emcha from its trap. Two Shermans, connected in series by tow cables and moving at slow speed, dragged the unfortunate vehicle out. One "transoceanic" [another nickname for the Sherman] could hardly have accomplished this difficult task alone. It could have easily found itself in a similar predicament. New operating methods, unknown in the West, were becoming our friends.

I ordered the battalion chief of staff, Guards Captain Nikolay Bogdanov, quickly to forward the appropriate report to the brigade commander concerning the obstacle we had encountered and how we overcame it. Our comrades-in-arms should not have to experience the same difficulties. "Your misfortune or combat success is passed quickly along to all the *Emchisti!*" Thus it was in past battles. This tradition continued also in the Far East!

This unanticipated delay of the 1st Battalion forced the brigade main body to halt. Now we had to make up for the lost time. Ahead of us was terrain that I thought would permit us to maintain a high rate of movement. In the saddle between the twin hills [both had the same elevation], the units should reach a dirt road. And then speed off to the southeast, toward Sin-Sume (Bayan-Khoshun-Sume). The distance was approximately one hundred kilometers. It was smooth on paper, but we forgot about the gullies, and the need to go through them. We were counting on quickly rushing to this populated area and in actuality had to crawl toward it all day on 9 August. There were several reasons.

The first problem was a disappointment. Our topographic maps, putting it mildly, did not correspond to the terrain. I would put their accuracy at about 70 percent. I had expected to find a secondary road leading to Sin-Sume. In actuality, there was no trace of it on the ground. It possibly did pass through here at some forgotten time. The ancient wind had done its dirty deed—it had created the sand dunes that now buried the cart track.

Passing beneath the shadows of the twin hills, the battalion's units came into an unusual area: the ridges of hills on the west with significant spot elevations and the same placer rising up in the east. They ran from southwest to northeast. A valley extended between these stony lines. It was about twenty kilometers wide at its upper end, about twelve kilometers wide in the middle, and at the lower end (on the approaches to Sin-Sume) again twenty kilometers wide. Nature had constructed a broad wind tunnel of original configuration. Powerful winds continuously roared through it. The most ancient partners—a constant hot, dry wind and the merciless scorching sun—had made the soil in this terrain a mixture of fine pebbles and almost powderlike, crumbly sand.

The battalion's lead tanks, having stumbled into this dry quagmire, naturally began to flounder and bogged down. This time the rescuers were squatting on their own bellies. Our only hope was self-recovery. Each Emcha had two five-meter tow cables. They went into use.[2] With the tanks in lower gears, our movement speed was drastically reduced.

Dawn began to appear. The sun quickly rose from behind the

spurs of the Grand Khingan. The higher it rose, the more fierce its rays became. The ground, cooled down during the night, quickly warmed. The tanks' tracks began to raise thick dust into the air. After several minutes, the driver-mechanics were half blinded. The danger of collisions between vehicles sharply increased. Our movement formation changed without any general order. The middle of the column, and then also the trail, began to move out to the right, trying to avoid driving into the dust cloud of the vehicles in front. The battalion deployed into a line. The favorable nature of the terrain permitted this parade formation.

The temperature was 40° Centigrade [104° Fahrenheit]. The Shermans' armor was like a burning skillet. It was impossible to touch the turret and hull with a bare hand. The motors began to overheat. We were forced to make a short halt, during which we cleaned dust from the radiators and topped off the coolant levels. Good maintenance procedures called for more time for the engines to cool. But in a combat situation, one cannot always wait. We opened the radiator caps, and fountains of boiling water spewed forth. Fortunately, appropriate safety procedures had been followed, and no one was scalded.

We came upon the improved dirt road marked on the map at the western slopes of Hill 1244 and increased speed. The road disappeared after just three kilometers. And then the same unhappy picture as before: fine gravel, shifting hot sand, unsteady ground underfoot, low gears, increased fuel expenditure. This was not particularly alarming because we had fuel in our tanks and had not yet touched our auxiliary drums.

Still another problem arose. We were sure it wasn't our last. Several *tankodesantniki* were suffering from the heat. This was no surprise. The perpetual sun was beating down on everyone and everything, and the powerful cooling fans drew the engine heat out of the hull and onto the armor. The soldiers were wearing steel pots, which also heated their heads. In a word, they were overheating, and not a little. It would have been nice to have had our winter wool caps. They would not have relieved the heat 100 percent but would have at least guaranteed some respite. Just the same, the tankers found a means to ease the situation for their combat brothers. Thanks to whoever designed the crew compartment of the Sherman, each vehicle carried two twenty-liter metal-lined canisters. I had given the instruction periodically to dampen the *desantnikis'* summer headgear in the water and then use them as an auxiliary liner under the helmet. The broad throat of the cannister permitted a soldier or officer freely to thrust his hand into it and wet his summer headgear and then wring it out a bit without spilling the valuable liquid. We did not have any sunstrokes on this day or on following days, even though the sun continued to show us no mercy.

With very slow steps, the brigade's units all reached Sin-Sume by the end of the day. The rubber covering of the tracks suffered the most during this fifty-kilometer sandy trek. It was almost completely stripped off of several track blocks. Deep splits and wounds were evident on the remaining track.

And so 130 of the most difficult kilometers were covered on the first day of the offensive. An order came down: cease movement. The extreme exhaustion of the personnel was evident. Our tracked and wheeled vehicles required maintenance. Bayan-Khoshun-Sume (Sin-Sume) was the first large inhabited locale on the axis of the 9th Guards Mechanized Corps' offensive. Staff officers had searched for this settlement for about an hour, but all they found was ruins, overgrown by a variety of vegetation. They could not find any water sources. We used the supplies we brought with us, carefully hoarding every drop.

We worked on the tanks with sweaty faces. We changed the air filters, removed a thin layer of dust from the honeycombs of the radiators, and threw away the bald track blocks. The driver-mechanics found the time for a four-hour rest. They knew that the difficulties that lay ahead had not diminished.

At this time, some groups of officers from the brigade staff (intelligence officers) at a salt-marshy plateau that stretched out up ahead found a bypass route around the countless marshes. They found the most trafficable axis—almost due south in the nomad territory of Tanto-Nur-Edo with a subsequent turn to the east to reach Korobonlin pass (benchmark 1298). The offensive was renewed at dawn on 10 August. The first thirty-five kilometers turned out to be particularly difficult. The sappers worked feverishly. They filled in marshy spots with sand and piles of stones and in a number of places even built wooden decking. The tanks moved slowly but without bogging down. A day later, when heavy rains began to fall, we were genuinely glad that they did not catch the units in the salt-marshy plateau.

By midday, the battalion had jumped "from the frying pan into the fire." The region around the Khingan Range was basically a sandy steppe, with localized areas of salt marsh. Before our tankers' eyes unfolded a multicolored carpet of many square kilometers. The unusual panorama of this desert terrain cast a spell over us for a time. Earlier, in June and then again in July, heavy rains had fallen here. Now, an enormous, almost limitless, area was covered with a brilliant, green-red-yellow "tablecloth." We hated to tear up this heretofore unseen beauty with our tracks. In wartime, however, the combat mission takes precedence! We moved on. A few score meters farther on, the desert once again displayed its capriciousness. Two Shermans got stuck.

It turned out that in this foothills area, it was dangerous for even two tanks to follow in one track. Unfortunately, the beautiful coverlet of the desert had a thickness of just several centimeters. And it barely supported the weight of even a single Emcha. The battalion deployed on line. We had to move not less than thirty kilometers in this formation.

By midday on 10 August, the main body of the 46th Guards Tank Brigade had reached the western slopes of the Grand Khingan Range. Our combat mission was accomplished a day earlier than specified.

Forward units of the neighboring 5th Guards Tank Corps also were pulling into the foothills of the Grand Khingan Range. The forces of the 6th Guards Army had stopped. We enjoyed a brief operational pause while we waited for the results of the reconnaissance of the passes.

In connection with the high tempo of the tank army's offensive, at noon on 10 August the commander of Transbaikal *Front* changed the deadline for the accomplishment of its immediate mission, requiring that it reach the Lubeya-Tutsyuan' line by the night of 12 August.

This short break in the action was used in the corps' units to prepare the equipment and personnel to overcome the mountain massif. We refueled the Shermans with our last onboard fuel supplies, carefully inspected the suspension components, and checked the tie-down straps on our self-recovery logs, pioneer tools, and fuel and water containers on the tanks. This was to prevent all this on-vehicle and supplementary exterior equipment from shifting around during the severe incline of the Emcha moving in the mountains. All the steering gear was inspected and adjusted, especially the braking systems.

Guards Lieutenant Colonel Pavel Shul'meyster assembled the battalion commanders. He relayed the results of two days of continuous advance. They rejoiced. Despite the complicated natural conditions, the tanks had survived this most difficult movement without accidents and serious breakdowns. The troops had courageously withstood their first enormous physical test.

The chief of the brigade's political section, Guards Lieutenant Colonel Valentin Yakimov, emphasized that the Guards *Dnestrovtsy* [from their brigade's honorific title "Dnester"] had coped exceptionally well with the assigned mission in the first phase of the offensive. He closed his brief speech with the parting words: "Ten different obstacles are behind us; thirty, perhaps no less insidious, lie ahead. Do not weaken your resolve!"

Valentin Dmitrievich was not mistaken in his suppositions.

In the Southern Reaches of the Grand Khingan

This was not the first time the Guards *Emchisti* had encountered mountains. We had conducted an offensive in the Transylvanian Alps [Romania] and fought with the enemy in northwestern Hungary. That experience, however, was clearly insufficient preparation for the exceptionally difficult natural conditions of the current offensive. In the southern reaches of the Grand Khingan we encountered many unfamiliar obstacles.

The night of 11 August. Dark, quiet, cool. At 0200, an intelligence report arrived—scouts had passed through Korobonlin Pass, detected no enemy, and were continuing to reconnoiter. Our neighboring 5th Guards Tank Corps had received a similar report somewhat earlier.

The army commander responded with originality to these reports: all the army and corps combat engineer units were ordered to move immediately forward to improve the routes through the passes. August was a period of monsoon winds that carried enormous masses of precipitation inland from the sea. Closer to dawn, rain suddenly poured down. From this time forward, heavy rains with brief interludes were our constant companion for many days.

At 0500, the brigade's units received the command to move out. Units of the 9th Guards Mechanized Corps were to pass through the range along the valleys of two rivers: 30th and 31st Guards Mechanized Brigades along the Suti Gol and 46th Tank and 18th Mechanized Brigades along the Taraleli Gol.

The Shermans climbed higher and higher with each kilometer. To the right and left, the mountain heights propped up a sky heavy with rain clouds, sending streaming torrents of rain crashing to the ground. The route lay along the southern slope of the northern heights. Tanks were moving in lower gears, with a constant list to the right side. In places, their lean reached a dangerous magnitude. At any moment, an Emcha could quickly fall on its side. This brought to my mind, and to the minds of several other veteran officers of the brigade, the wistful days of December '43 in Ukraine. How easily the *lend lizi* [another nickname for the Shermans, from Lend-Lease] toppled over. The tracks sprayed sodden dirt; under its fifteen-centimeter layer was solid rock. In particularly dangerous sectors, the tanks moved at walking speed. Indeed, in these conditions, "Move slower, go farther!" was an appropriate caution.

The rain continued to lash us. Everywhere we looked was a dense curtain of water. The crews and *desantniki* were drenched to the bone. But they did not lose their spirit. They even joked with each other: "We survived the dry, hot desert, now a new test—water. Patience, lads, patience! The Asian monsoons are rich in cloudbursts!"

Finally, we crawled forward to Korobonlin Pass, 1,298 meters [4,063 feet] above sea level. We had climbed almost to the heavens. It was not a heartwarming sight, however: a gentle climb and a steep, narrow descent. Corps combat engineers and recovery assets had been set up here for some time. They were prepared to get the tanks up over the hump of one of the southern reaches of the range.

We struggled here for many hours. Two-tracked recovery vehicles, rigged together, were parked in the pass. The lead vehicle with the winch was the "mule," and the second assumed the role of "anchor," holding the winching vehicle in place.

The Shermans were winched through the pass one at a time in the following manner. The steel winch cable from the "mule" was secured to the rear towing pintle of the first tank in the file. The tank moved under its own power, in first gear. Behind it, the tight "leash" [winch cable] slowly uncoiled. This reliable precaution prevented the tank from careening out of control on the steep downslope.

Our wheeled vehicles negotiated Korobonlin Pass in the same fashion, with a slight variation. Tens of soldiers walked alongside each truck, helping to keep it on the path.

After the pass, the brigade's units forded the Taraleli Gol River and then advanced along its left bank. The trail followed a narrow canyon for approximately thirty kilometers. At times, it seemed that the battalion would fall over the rocky precipice. Heavy rain clouds hung over our heads, pouring hundreds of liters of water on us every minute. The air was so oversaturated with exhaust gases that breathing was difficult. And despite all this, we maintained our positive outlook. We were moving forward, albeit slowly. The terrain itself protected us from the threat of enemy air attacks. All the tankers' attention was focused on "ground" concerns—to keep their Emchas upright. In addition, the canyon turned out to be stopped up for several hours.

With each kilometer of movement to the southeast, the Shermans' engines worked with less strain. We began our descent from the high mountain plateau. The valley of the Taraleli Gol River began gradually to broaden out. The tanks increased their speed somewhat. Until this time, they had not exceeded five to six kilometers per hour.

On one of the small downward inclines in the trail, the deteriorated surface became the cause of an accident, fortunately without serious consequences. One of the trailing Shermans braked sharply. The vehicle did not stop but quickly slid down the hill on its locked, rubber-soled tracks, as if on skis. Several seconds later, the sliding tank overtook the Emcha moving in front of it and collided with it, the main gun of the sliding tank striking the moving tank in the rear. The trailing tank's main gun recoiled fully.

After careful inspection of the gun, the battalion chief of armaments, Guards Senior Lieutenant Ivan Korchak, reported to me that he found no damage. Just as a precaution, he requested permission to fire one round. He intended to use this crude method to check the serviceability of the gun. In those field conditions, we had no other choice. A similar situation had never before occurred in my almost three years at the front. We did not want to be in a state of ignorance relative to the combat capability of this tank. I gave my "OK" to the test fire, but only with a solid-shot round. We rotated the turret to the north, put maximum elevation on it, and fired. The recoil mechanism functioned properly. It is good when an accident has such a fortunate outcome. Our solid shot has rested for nearly fifty years somewhere in the mountains of the Grand Khingan.

We moved onward. From above, rain poured and poured as from a fire hose. The trail came to the Taraleli Gol River, to a fording site. Both banks of the river were in a broad expanse of swamp. It would not be so simple to cross this water obstacle. About ten sappers were hardening the marshy ground at the banks with rocks. The scope of the task was so great, and there were so few of them. A bulldozer had been called forward to assist, but it might be some time in arriving. Another delay, perhaps more than an hour. We had to break out of this "stone corridor" [the rock road] quickly. I left only the driver-mechanics on the tanks and ordered the remaining crew members and *desantniki* to reinforce the tired sappers. The latter became the advisers, telling our tankers what, where, and how to lay in the rocks.

The men proceeded with good spirits. They began to fill in especially marshy spots with our now superfluous empty water cans, filling them with small stones and sand. We quickly prepared about one hundred meters of backfilled trail on the near shore and a bit less on the far shore. We sent one Sherman forward to test the road. It carefully approached the river in first gear, slowly forded across, and, without increasing speed, crawled forward to a hard spot, where it stopped.

Tankers and *desantniki* stood on both sides of the rock- and gravel-backfilled road with shovels and tankers' bars [crowbars]. As soon as the first vehicle passed, they quickly filled in the holes that appeared in the just-passed-over ruts.

After all the Emchas successfully crossed the river, the battalion passed the baton to the brigade's other unit [2d Battalion].

Now they would have to expend some effort to overcome this same river. Our column surged to the southeast. After approximately fifteen kilometers, we reached a broader floodplain of the Taraleli Gol. Villages began to appear, bordered by the small patches of fields. Mature *gaolyan* [a type of sorghum] and *chumiza* [a green bristle grass] were standing in them like a wall. These combined cereal grasses, as we later learned, were a staple of the Chinese and Manchurian diet. For some time, at least two years, we would be eating *kasha* [porridge] made from *gaolyan* and *chumiza*.[1]

The "water bombing" continued. The Shermans carefully struggled along the trail that lay near the foothill of one of the high mountains of the eastern reaches of the range. As before, there existed a real danger that one of the tanks would overturn, this time to the left side.

On the afternoon of 11 August, the brigade's units were approaching the confluence of the two rivers, the Taraleli Gol and the Dalaerkhe. By this time, our reconnaissance had determined that the conditions for crossing this obstacle were very difficult. As a result of the floods from the rains, a significant sector of the approaches to the rivers was under water. The ground was saturated. We needed embankments [as in a railroad or roadbed] and bridges. We could be halted here for more than a day. In addition, the tanks would again have to negotiate a "stone tunnel" [another rock road] on the other side of the river and move at reduced speeds.

The scouts found and checked out a bypass around this choke point: a turn to the south along the valley of the Taraleli Gol, then to the east along the Khukhur Gol River. The route was somewhat longer but better in a number of ways. It would facilitate the subsequent movement of the column by avoiding one of the eastern reaches of the range that had a height of one thousand meters above sea level. The terrain on this route was somewhat inhabitable—there were signs of small villages along the road. The cart tracks between them would permit us to maintain an adequate march speed. This report also heartened the corps operations staff officers traveling with the brigade. East of Khan'myao, sappers were completing the construction of a forty-five-ton bridge across the Khukhur Gol River. In a word, the problem of overcoming the last river line in the southern reaches of the range had been resolved.

Without delay, the brigade's units hurried southward at a speed of twelve to fifteen kilometers per hour. We quickly reached the populated area Khan'myao, which was large by local standards. Engineer traffic control troops directed the tanks to their high-capacity bridge. On the opposite bank of the Khukhur Gol, the road also permitted us to hold a good speed. Finally, in another twenty kilometers, the Shermans broke out onto the plain that stretched all the way to the city of Lubeya. By the end of 11 August, the 46th Guards Brigade had reached this first city in the corps' offensive zone. And then stopped. The fuel cells of our Emchas were empty. Not a drop of fuel remained in our auxiliary tanks or fuel cans either. The difficult road conditions in the southern reaches of the Grand Khingan had required more than twice the forecasted POL [petroleum, oils, and lubricants]. Because of the unending deluges of rain, the supplying of fuel to the wheeled vehicles had been almost totally stopped.

And so the forces of the 6th Guards Tank Army had concluded the second phase of the offensive, no less arduous than the first. Three days of the operation had passed. Behind us remained the stone giant [the Grand Khingan]. The surprise and rapid seizure of the mountain passes through the Grand Khingan, which was considered to be unsuitable for the actions of large troop formations and modern combat equipment, deprived the Japanese command of the ability to use this important strategic position for organizing a strong defense. The main body of the 9th Mechanized and 5th Tank Guards Corps had reached the central Manchurian plain in the area of Lubeya, having accomplished their mission on the fifth day of the operation.

Help from the Air Transports

The situation at the end of the third day of the operation required the development of a rapid offensive from the forces of the Transbaikal *Front*, especially the armored-mechanized forces, to complete the defeat of the main body of the Kwantung Army and prevent its withdrawal into northern Korea and to Lyaodung Peninsula.

However, the accomplishment of this mission was totally dependent on the supplying of fuel to the 6th Guards Tank Army formations. The army's logistic units were far behind and their supply routes long (the supply point in Tamsag-Bulak city was approximately seven hundred kilometers away). In addition, heavy rains had made the roads and tracks across the Grand Khingan impassable for all wheeled vehicles. Immediate assistance was required. And it arrived.

The *front* commander, Marshal of the Soviet Union R. Ya. Malinovskiy, activated two air transport divisions of the 12th Air Army to deliver fuel to General A. G. Kravchenko's tankers. They flew 160 to 170 aircraft sorties daily. In contemporary terminology, an "air bridge" was organized, which operated continuously from 10 to 22 August. During this time, transport aircraft delivered 940 tons of POL products. Despite its considerable demands, the army was far from completely satisfied.

Consequently, General Kravchenko made a decision that fundamentally changed the method of operation of his tank formations. From 12 August onward, responsibility for the accomplishment of the primary missions now belonged to the strong forward detachments of the 5th Guards Tank and 7th Mechanized Corps. These detachments were supplied with the necessary diesel fuel. The first to receive fuel were the reconnaissance units of these two corps, which were required to conduct ground reconnaissance to great depth. The 9th Guards Mechanized Corps was in the army's second echelon at the start of the offensive in the central Manchurian plain. It was to move behind the 5th [Guards] Stalingrad Tank Corps.

The 9th Corps units began to receive fuel on the afternoon of 15 August. The heavens showed us some mercy. The intensity of the rain lessened somewhat. Patches of open sky, which the air transporters used for flights into the tank army formations' dispositions, began to appear more often. The flat terrain south of Lubeya permitted the Douglases [c-47s] to land not far from our 46th Brigade. The cargo compartments of these aircraft were packed tight with fuel drums. The crews quickly pushed them out onto the ground and rolled them to their tanks. We did not have pumps to transfer the diesel into the Shermans' fuel cells. The quite suitable canvas pails that were included in each vehicle's on-board equipment came to the rescue.

On this day, sufficient fuel was delivered to fill the primary fuel cells only half full. The pilots promised to deliver more diesel on the morning of 16 August, weather permitting.

I and the commander of the 2d Battalion decided to "sweeten the pot" for the aviators. On the first day of the offensive, we had picked up a large flock of sheep discarded by the fleeing Japanese in the Gobi Desert. This meat on the hoof, which was being used as a food supply for the tankers and *desantniki*, had safely withstood all the trials along the difficult road traveled by the brigade's units. During the battalions' stay at Lubeya, the size of the flock had diminished noticeably, but many still remained.

Going another step in that direction, we decided to "kill two birds with one stone": to stake out the next fuel delivery for ourselves by presenting the aviators a generous gift and, at the same time, ridding ourselves of this unusual, somewhat troublesome burden. In the near future, the *Emchisti* would have to move hurriedly to Tunlyao and then on to Mukden. Engagements with the enemy were a possibility. To keep the Shermans in an undersupplied condition any longer was fraught with serious difficulties, including the disruption of the accomplishment of our combat mission.

We ordered our adjutants to make the aviators aware of the desires of we two battalion commanders. And simultaneously, to reach an agreement with them on the time of loading the live cargo into their aircraft. Our suggestion was warmly received.

The tankers, having quickly rolled the emptied fuel drums to the aircraft, jokingly called to the air transporters: "Take these empty drums, and a gift from us . . . a pair of sheep." They loaded four to six animals into each Douglas.

The fifth night at Lubeya passed. As the sky reddened in the east, we heard the roar of aircraft motors approaching from the northwest. Undoubtedly, the air transports were flying toward us.

Sometime around 0900 on 16 August, all the tanks' fuel cells were filled to the top. The aviators gave us *nazemniki* [literally, "ground people"] a hearty thanks from all their maintenance and support personnel for this priceless gift. And they reported that today a "king's feast" awaited them. We bade farewell to the fuel deliverers very warmly, wishing each other combat success on the front-line roads.

The aircraft took a northward course, and the Sherman tanks moved to the southeast.

On the Central Manchurian Plain

Dropping down out of the mountains, the tankers rejoiced that they finally had broken loose from the "mouth of the dragon." They could see farther and breathe easier on the plain. As we later learned, our joy was somewhat premature. Our difficulties were not yet over. In comparison with our previous trials, they were twice or even three times worse. In other words, the severe testing of the Shermans and the verifying of their crews' endurance and courage would continue. On the first day of our movement toward Tunlyao, the soldiers expressed their attitude toward the developing situation with the words: "You are a broad valley, but we hate you!"

During the course of the march, each kilometer cost us immense effort and twice the norm of fuel. The rains stopped briefly, permitting us to admire the limitless crops of succulent grasses, then again pelted our faces with torrents of water. The road surface became a thick porridgelike mash. In places, the tanks created a muddy bow wave ahead of them. We had to take the 160-kilometer distance to Tunlyao "by storm" over the course of more than two days. No consideration was given to maneuvering around difficult sectors of the route or increasing speed. For everywhere one looked, it was swampy fields and, on the road, a meter of fermenting mud! The Emchas' motors were stressed to the limit. They withstood the enormous strain well; not one broke down.

Having crossed the Silyaokhe River by bridge, the brigade's units drew up to the western outskirts of Tunlyao on the morning of 19 August. This was the second large city on our route. It became, in its own right, the jumping-off point for an unusual and most difficult march.

Something unbelievable happened here. The roads leading from Tunlyao to the southeast were unsuitable even for the movement of tanks. The several days of pouring rain had turned the broad central Manchurian plain into a kind of artificial lake. In this critical situation, when each hour was precious, a uniquely practicable decision was made, to cross this submerged terrain on the narrow embankment of the railroad bed, from Tunlyao to Chzhanu and beyond to Mukden. The total length of this "cross-tie road" was approximately 250 kilometers.

I remember that day well. When the chain of command's decision was announced, several of us veteran officers were somewhat alarmed. We understood too well that such a risky step was not taken on a whim. Two corps (5th Tank and 9th Mechanized) would be moving along a single slender thread. "He who has not fought in war does not know what risk is!" This is true. We wondered how many "hidden boulders" were on this lifesaving, and dangerous, route.

It would be twice as difficult for the army's second-echelon units, that is to say, for us, the *inomarochniki* [foreign-vehicle tankers], to move along the fairly well broken-up railroad embankment. We had no doubts about this whatsoever. The rugged track system of the thirty-two-ton T-34 had left the embankment in just such a condition. The Sherman was four tons heavier than the Soviet tank. This had to be taken into account.

In such difficult march conditions, we had to forget about movement speed. We traveled at a walking pace. This meant an increased expenditure of priceless diesel fuel. At the same time, this also rendered the slow-moving Emcha a good target for Japanese air attacks.

As my native Ukrainians say, "It was considered, it was proposed, but when it came down to business—not everything went well!"

The 46th Brigade spent all of several hours in Tunlyao. The crews managed to perform maintenance on their Shermans. A long and difficult road lay ahead of them. I must say that this eleventh day of the operation turned out to be quite eventful. The 21st Guards Tank Brigade of 5th Corps had captured the city of Chzhanu by the morning of 19 August. Air-landed infantry captured the large cities of Chan'chun and Mukden. Units of the 9th Mechanized Corps had to hurry onward.

The brigade's tanks drove up onto the railroad embankment south of Tunlyao. We began the march across the railroad cross ties. This continued for two days. All sorts of things occurred along this route. From the first meters, we felt the "charm" of the sole dry strip of ground. The ends of the ties were heavily splintered. Deep gouges remained from the tracks of the 5th Tank Corps' T-34 tanks, moving ahead of us in the first echelon. The T-34, with a somewhat wider stance than a Sherman, moved with the rails between its tracks. The Emchas were not able to do this. We had to drive with one track between the rails and the other on the gravel ballast of the ties. In doing this, the tank leaned significantly to the side. We had to move more than one hundred kilometers in this lopsided attitude. In addition, the vehicles vibrated on the ties as though they were in convulsions. It was especially difficult when we encountered bridges. We had to go around them. To do so, we had to prepare dismounting and mounting points to get down off of and back onto the embankment. And all of this with the efforts of our crews and *desantniki*. True, we had all the brigade's units.

At 1700 on 19 August, my 1st Battalion—the lead unit in the column—reached Bakhuta siding. Here stood one modest brick building. The rain had stopped a short time earlier. The *Emchisti* and *tankodesantniki* were removing their wet clothing. As before, the water was all around us. An unusual engagement occurred at this point along our route of march.

Observers loudly shouted out, "Air!" The gun commanders

in the crews rushed to their covered antiaircraft machine guns. For several days now, we had protected them from the heavy precipitation. During the brief interludes between rains, they remained in the travel position. Until now enemy aircraft had never bothered us. Now, six spots had appeared on the horizon, fighter-bombers hurriedly approaching from the south. Our Westerners had mastered well the tactics of German pilots. Before they dropped their bombs, they circled over the target. They selected the aiming point, and only after this, the leader turned his aircraft into a dive. But here, everything unfolded according to a different scenario. Events developed so rapidly that we did not even have time to bring our machine guns into action. How did this unusual Japanese attack conclude?

The first aircraft raced toward the battalion's lead tank at low altitude. And at full speed, it plowed into the tank's hull. Pieces of the fuselage flew off in all directions. The airplane's engine buried itself under the tank's tracks. Tongues of flame licked around the Sherman's hull. The driver-mechanic, Guards Sergeant Nikolay Zuev, received numerous cuts and bruises.

The *desantniki* from the first three tanks ran into the brick building to seek cover. The second Japanese pilot guided his aircraft into this structure. Crashing through the roof, it lodged itself in the attic. None of our soldiers were injured. It immediately became clear: kamikaze were attacking our battalion.

The third pilot did not repeat the mistake of his comrades. He dropped sharply toward the ground and flew his aircraft toward a window of the building. He also was unable to reach his target. His wing caught a telegraph pole, and the fighter-bomber crashed into the ground. It quickly burst into flames.

The fourth aircraft dived on the column. It crashed into a truck belonging to the battalion aid station, setting it on fire. The last two kamikaze directed their attack at the column's trailing tanks and were met by a dense curtain of antiaircraft fire. Struck by machine-gun bursts, both aircraft crashed into the water not far from the railroad embankment. The air attack had lasted several brief moments. Six fighter-bombers were turned into shapeless heaps of metal, with six dead pilots. What really surprised us, however, were the female corpses in the cockpits of two of the aircraft. In all likelihood, these were fiancées of the kamikaze pilots, who had decided to share the dismal fate of their selected ones. Our losses were insignificant: one truck burned, a gouged turret on the lead Sherman, and one driver-mechanic disabled. We quickly pushed the truck off into the water, sat the assistant driver-mechanic behind the controls of the tank, and continued the march.

With the approach of nightfall, we were hoping for a rest. The tankers were very tired. Some of them had not slept for days. The vibration on the ties was especially exhausting. But a categorical order arrived: "Continue to march!" The situation demanded it. We were given permission to turn on our headlights. Low beams. Despite this, we moved at only twenty to twenty-five kilometers per hour. On grades and hills, our speed was reduced to half of that.

By the morning of 20 August, we were having a problem. Frankly, we knew that sooner or later this would happen. We were only unable to foresee the nature of the problem. The suspension components were unable to withstand the enormous overloading and began to deform. Then the buffer springs of the bogie wheel suspension arms broke. This occurred on three Shermans, bringing to mind August 1944, when the Emchas became "barefooted" in the Jassy-Kishinev operation. In this case, another "illness" of the same suspension system. We had to let off the gas and move at a snail's pace. The march continued at this reduced tempo.

By the middle of the day, the brigade's units had reached Chzhanu. Here, to the great joy of the tankers and *desantniki*, we abandoned the railway and drove along the concrete. We immediately increased our speed to the maximum—just under fifty kilometers per hour. Even the lame tanks did not fall behind. Ninety minutes later, the column was once again forced to straddle the hated railroad tracks. It was sixty vibrating kilometers to Mukden.

The tankers had experienced much on the long journey from the forward assembly area: they scorched in the heat, bogged down in the desert sands, forced a track through the mountains (every minute risking a rollover), ate dust for several consecutive days, and washed it down with torrents of rain. It would seem that everyone had been driven to the brink. But no! A new problem arose—another obstacle. We had to cross the Lyaokhe River on a railroad bridge. This would be no simple matter. The listing Shermans did not fit between the [low] sides of the bridge structure. We had to streamline the vehicle. I thought about it, and the company commanders and battalion staff sought a solution. We discussed various ideas. The best of these was to load the Emchas on platform cars and move them to the opposite bank.

We had to find platform cars, even just two or three. And a steam engine. We created two groups of scouts to go out and find the necessary equipment. One group was sent back to the station we had recently passed through, the second to the next station ahead. After about an hour, discomforting news reached us. Platform cars of only sixteen tons capacity had been found, but no locomotives. Another (it was difficult to count which one of the many since the beginning of the offensive) difficulty.

There was one way out: we had to push these loaded platform cars across the bridge by hand. A Herculean task, for sure. We constructed a loading platform out of various makeshift materials and maneuvered a single tank onto two platform cars. A team of twenty men was assigned to each platform. Their strength was sufficient to push and to hold the valuable cargo on grades. The first shuttle was successful, but it took almost four hours. The axle boxes smoked from the inordinate overloading. We took various measures, such as pouring diesel fuel and oil on the bearings. And again we put them under the load.

The sweat poured off our arms. Our hands bled from pushing and dragging all the Shermans to the opposite bank of the Lyao-khe River. We breathed a sigh of relief, then moved off toward Mukden. On the morning of 21 August, we reached its northwestern outskirts. The order came down to halt in the city.

Mukden

How long would we be in Mukden? At the time we still did not know that this was the final stop on the offensive advance by units of the 9th Guards Mechanized Corps. The 5th Guards Tank Corps continued to advance to Port Arthur and Dal'nya.[1]

It was still wartime. We had just arrived in this now liberated city. We did not exclude the possibility that in the city we would encounter kamikaze soldiers and others, already in civilian clothes, fanatics, or common soldiers. We had to maintain, as they say, a sharp lookout.

The brigade commander set aside two parallel streets for the battalion's "parking lot." They were separated by a square. Georgiy Danil'chenko's company occupied the square. The tanks of Dmitriy Niyakiy parked along the curbs of the second street.

The crews had all been strictly ordered to remain with their vehicles. They were to hold their main guns and machine guns in readiness for combat. Anything might happen.

When the battalion had been in Mukden for about two hours, we were alerted. We received the mission to disarm a Japanese tank unit in a nearby sector of the city. The five-kilometer road march required little time. We reached the objective: a military garrison of a Japanese tank brigade. We encircled it with our Shermans, their main guns and machine guns loaded. We were ordered to open fire on the garrison at the slightest sign of resistance.

A parliamentary group was formed comprising the battalion chief of staff, Captain Nikolay Bogdanov, an interpreter, and two sergeants. All were armed. The group walked toward the enemy bastion under a white flag. Not more than thirty tense minutes had passed when the parliamentarians finally emerged through the compound's gates. A Japanese officer was coming out with them.

The Japanese officer—a captain, with anger in his voice— reported to me in perfect Russian that they had received an order from their own command to surrender their arms. "What procedure do you wish us to follow?" he asked me.

We gave the following instructions to the Japanese officer: to surrender all small arms; where to drive and park the tanks and other combat vehicles; and where, after this had been accomplished, to assemble all the soldiers. Bogdanov also drew him a sketch indicating the locations of these points. The Japanese captain indicated his understanding of the instructions and returned to his unit. We worriedly waited the fulfillment of our requirements. Brigade and corps staff officers arrived to observe the activity, and I briefed them on the situation.

About an hour passed in waiting. As before, all was quiet in the compound. The *Emchisti* were ready for anything. Suddenly, it was as if the Japanese were preparing for their last engagement. Inside the compound we heard the racing of tank engines. A light truck quickly appeared in the gates. Behind it followed several staff buses and then the tanks. It was a brigade column. The lead tank came up to my Sherman and stopped. I was handed the TOE [table of organization and equipment] for the brigade, in Russian. This was a great surprise to us. It was clearly the work of the captain-negotiator.

The commanding officers of the units were the first to lay down their weapons. They immediately were seated in two light vehicles and taken to corps headquarters under guard.

For almost the remainder of the day we accepted the capitulation of the Japanese tankers. Fairness requires me to note that even in this difficult, disgraceful period, the officers, noncommissioned officers, and soldiers carried out every instruction regarding surrender of their weapons and equipment. Military discipline was maintained to the last fateful moment, when all of the more than one thousand assigned soldiers of the brigade became prisoners of war. The final command was issued in Japanese and the former tankers, under heavy guard, marched off into Mukden, to a prisoner-of-war collection point.

I turned to the captain who had negotiated for the Japanese command with a question. "Captain, where did you learn Russian so well?" Standing quietly for a moment, he replied, with some assertiveness in his voice, "It was my duty."

Upon completion of all the procedures of accepting the Japanese capitulation, I and the other officers of the battalion command were sent to confirm, first of all, the actual number of tanks as compared to the paperwork we had been handed. Of course, any staff clerk could have accomplished this task. But I must honestly admit that we wanted to see the Japanese tanks up close. Our professional curiosity took priority. The armored vehicles were more suited to colonial campaigns than serious war fighting.

"Captain, how did you intend to fight against Soviet T-34s and American Shermans with such tanks as these?" I asked the Japanese captain-parliamentarian.

Not concealing his enormous hatred toward us, the Japanese officer responded, "Captain, had there been a confrontation, had we seen your five thousand tanks, we would have found twelve thousand soldiers willing to sacrifice themselves."[2] It seemed to me that there was a kernel of irrefutable truth in the words of this defeated enemy. The point of his remark was the weapon he named. It could be said that a well-organized employment of this tactic could have had disastrous effects on our force. This was something that we had to acknowledge.

Concerning his words, "had there been a confrontation," he, perhaps, had in mind the capitulation order. But for it, the Japanese would still be fighting. It was said that the beloved emperor himself gave the order.

This brought to mind an old Russian proverb: "After a fistfight, one should not brandish his fists." The officer of the Land of the Rising Sun decided thus to brandish his fists after losing the fight. He might have been surprised by the outcome.

The Japanese forces moved rapidly toward their fate. Garrison after garrison, position upon position laid down their arms. The Kwantung Army, like snow before the sun, melted away by the day, by the hour.

Victory over Japan Day occurred on 3 September. To us it was almost like any other day. It did not evoke that torrent of joy we felt on 9 May in the West. That victory (in Europe) had been eagerly anticipated for 1,418 days and nights. This one took less than a month. Here, in the Far East, "soldiers' salutes" with every kind of weapon, as were fired in honor of the victory over Germany, did not break the quiet of the night. It was nothing like that.

Yes, another enemy had been defeated. Of course, everyone was happy. We saluted the victors, but modestly, on a smaller scale, in all our units. Thus there were no large celebrations or fireworks. Eyewitnesses recounted that the sailors of the Pacific Fleet greeted the victory achieved in the Far East with boundless enthusiasm. This was their first victory and in a difficult operation. It would be shameful to criticize them.

Celebratory meals and meetings were conducted in units. The soldiers received twice their normal ration of vodka.[3]

On 5 September, the 46th Guards Tank Brigade received instructions: leave one crew member on each tank, officers fall out. The remainder of the enlisted men loaded foodstuffs found in warehouses of the Japanese supply depots onto rail boxcars. The goods included rice, *chumiza*, *gaolyan*, various locally canned goods, and summer and winter clothing of the defeated Kwantung Army. In other words, confiscated war booty. Our men worked at this task for five days. And when the brigade commander became aware of the scope of the work required, he shook his head. It had become clear that the number of tankers assigned to the task could not accomplish the work in the required time. The only solution was to turn to local nationals in Mukden. About five hundred locals began to show up for work each day. Their pay—in kind. They received a portion of whatever they were loading. The arrangement was reported to the corps commander. The response from him was "I approve."

On this same day, in the Mukden bazaar, our interpreter made an announcement concerning hiring for temporary work, indicating the number of workers needed on a daily basis and the manner of payment. On 6 September, there was a sea of people outside the gates of the supply dump.

The required number of civilians were admitted and divided into teams of ten persons each with an appointed leader. Now the *Emchisti* worked as supervisors of the local populace in loading the supplies into the boxcars and filling out the proper transportation documents. We admired the coordinated work effort of the Chinese and Manchurians and delighted in the rapidity of their actions. A human conveyor was formed at each boxcar. At times it appeared that the sacks and boxes were themselves running along the backs and hands of the loaders. And so it went every day. The wagons were quickly loaded to their capacity, secured, and pushed by hand onto a siding.

I don't remember exactly if it was the seventh or eighth of September that something extraordinary happened. In a far corner of the supply dump we found some crates, large cartons with medical supplies and bandages. I immediately sent the battalion *feldsher* to the brigade doctor to report our findings. This discovery was indeed a priceless find.

The attention of all my subordinates immediately turned to this warehouse. They began to discover medicinal alcohol in it. We had quickly to issue a warning to all the seekers. True, the *Emchisti* were able to discover pieces of something like soap in one of the fifteen or twenty crates. For us "greasers," this was a find. They were very happy and began to wash their hands with this "soap." But it did not clean their hands. The tankers cursed and became upset. Then they threw the "soap" away. They remembered a similar German "trophy." The Germans had ersatz soap that lathered up the same way. The Japanese was even worse.

Some of the locals working in the supply dump asked our soldiers for these "soap" bars. Acceding to the wishes of the Mukden locals, we handed them out with delight. What value did they find in these hard lumps?

The brigade and corps medical staff arrived. I explained to them what was happening and why I had disturbed them. I told them about the Japanese "soap" that did not clean anything. My battalion maintenance officer, Guards Captain Aleksandr Dubitskiy, held one of the topics of our conversation in his hand. Guards Lieutenant Colonel of Medical Service Nikolay Karpenko—the corps surgeon—almost in an exasperated voice, shouted: "Loza, post a guard! Don't you know what this is?"

"No, I don't."

"These are pieces of gold!"

We looked at each other, clearly not understanding what the doctor was saying.

"This is opium! The Japanese medical personnel used it for an analgesic."

Aleksandr Dubitskiy quickly secreted a piece of the substance in his pocket.

This humorous story concluded when a handbill was drawn up and the "priceless material" was carried to the corps medical battalion, along with countless medications, bandages, and so on.

Farewell, Emcha

It is not my desire, but I have no choice except to close this story of the Sherman tanks on a painful note. I have laid out the truth, and only the truth, on these many pages. It is with some sadness that I write the final truth.

A year had passed since the end of the war in the Far East. My wartime comrades were putting their peacetime lives together.

Some were out having a good time, others were thinking of getting married, and I decided to continue my education by attending a military academy. I submitted a request and then began feverishly to prepare for the entrance examination, using my regular leaves for this purpose.

At the moment of my return to the unit from leave, we received an unusual order: prepare the Sherman tanks for loading on rail platform cars. Without crews. Without ammunition. With one-fourth of a tank of fuel. The battalion was to form a team of fifteen men to accompany the tanks. As I recall, they explained that in accordance with the Lend-Lease agreement, all combat and transport equipment that remained in units after the end of the war was to be returned to the country of origin, or it could be paid for. The higher military chain of command in Moscow chose the first variant: to turn the foreign equipment over to American representatives arriving on sea transports at Vladivostok.

Two weeks were allocated for the preparation of the tanks for shipment. We had much to do during this time: bring the Emchas up to full combat readiness (they had been parked out in the open); correct all deficiencies (incidentally, the suspension systems damaged on the Manchurian railroad embankment had been repaired immediately upon the brigade's return to the Soviet Union); where necessary, paint the hulls and turrets; and ensure that each vehicle had every single item of on-board equipment and supplies.

In short, we had to make these Shermans look like they had just come through the gate of the tank plant. A most difficult task. Keep in mind that these tanks had traveled approximately fifteen hundred kilometers under their own power in the Manchurian operation and another 120 to 150 miles during the year of peacetime training.

Such is life. But as we all know, an order is an order. They are not discussed but unswervingly carried out. The crews did everything within their abilities. They prepared their Emchas for the long journey with dedication. When it was necessary, brigade mechanics came down to the battalion and quickly repaired a detected deficiency. A technical committee was created by special order of the tank brigade commander. During the period of work, this committee began to inspect the condition of each Sherman.

Serious deficiencies that had not been detected, and some small ones, were energetically repaired. The brigade command reported the full readiness of the tanks for movement.

Several days passed in anticipation of the order for loading. We had to say farewell to the Emchas. It would be a sad moment. We had wished it would be otherwise. A funereal parting, a great pain.

Finally, an order arrived. But with other, stunning contents, that sent chills running up and down our spines: "Remove the turrets and hull machine guns from the Shermans. Warehouse them. Deliver the armored hulls—as tractors—to civilian enterprises." We had to report compliance with this order within five days.

Why, for what reason, from where did such an abrupt change in the subsequent fate of the foreign tanks come? What forced Moscow to take such a final ["murderous" in original text] decision?

For days after receipt of the "death certificate" (as the tankers nicknamed the order), work proceeded on a broad front. All the brigade, corps, and army maintenance units were thrown into the demilitarization of the tanks, making "tractors" out of them.

I cannot forget the total dejectedness of the crews as they stood on the sidelines with heads bowed. The death of each tank showed on their faces. At one time, the *Emchisti* had signed hand receipts for the tanks from the brigade command. We all were heavy-hearted. Many choked back tears, and some, not holding back, cried bitterly. How could this be? How much effort and energy had been given to them—the Shermans—there in the dry Mongolian steppe, in the silent desert sands of the Gobi, in the rugged southern reaches of the Grand Khingan? And how many obstacles had been overcome on the central Manchurian plain? These men had cared for them, cared for them like the apple of their eye. And now this final humiliation. Farewell, Emcha! Each *inomarochnik* will have good memories of you for the rest of his life.

An epitaph came out of these mournful days (how could it not): "Yesterday it was a menacing tank, and now, by order—they took off the turret—it has become a tractor. Front-line comrade, how painful to witness the death of the Emcha. Try not to cry!"

The Sherman tractors of the 1st Battalion were sent to the Krasnoyarsk area [3,400 kilometers east of Moscow, in Siberia] for work in the forest industry, to clean snowdrifts from the roads (they pulled heavy metal v-plows). The vehicles were shipped in three groups, accompanied by our driver-mechanics and commanded by an officer.

Sometime a month or two after the "burial" of the Shermans, a rumor (perhaps false) reached us about why we had to "destroy" the foreign tanks. According to this rumor, Stalin himself made the decision. This was entirely possible. It was essentially a political issue. Hardly anyone else had the authority to make such a decision.

The essence of the rumor was that the American representatives in Vladivostok requested first of all that aircraft be taken aboard the ships. The Soviet side began to implement this request. American Lend-Lease fighters and bombers ferried from the Baltic and Transbaikal areas began to land at Far Eastern airfields. The ships took the first party of fighter aircraft aboard. In full view, the Americans placed the fighters directly into a powerful crusher. Our pilots could hardly believe their eyes. The "alloy pancakes" were then loaded into the holds. When its holds were full, the transport raised anchor and departed for the open sea, where it threw the unwanted scrap metal overboard. The emptied vessel appeared again at the dock.

Flash message traffic flew from the Far Eastern ground forces and naval military commands to Moscow. The fate of the Shermans was decided at the highest Kremlin cabinet level.

Countless hundreds of Emchas were on hand in Red Army units. In a five-day period, they all disappeared. They ceased to exist as a combat entity. They were written off at headquarters, and the matter ended. For more than a year, the Sherman turrets were preserved in motor pools. After the formations were demobilized, the turrets were carted away to weapons storage facilities.

Epilogue

I parted company with the Shermans long, long ago. But I have never forgotten them, not for a minute. Did I want to forget? Hardly!

Except for perhaps one month on a T-34, all of my time at the front was spent on foreign-made tanks. I saw it all: some were knocked out of action, some were blown up, and one burned. I avoided one misfortune—drowning. But I was "chopped down," one can say, "symmetrically." My Matilda was hit in September 1943, and I was seriously wounded in the right leg.[1] In April 1945, an antitank round fired from close range by a Tiger penetrated my attacking Sherman. Spalling from my own tank smashed into my left knee.

They discussed amputating my leg at the field hospital. Fortunately, the chief surgeon of the Second Ukrainian *Front*, Professor General Nikolay Nikolayevich Elanskiy, was at the hospital. This magician did the most complicated operation on me, reconstructing an almost primitive leg from shattered bone. I spent three months in recovery, more than half of it immobilized in a plaster cast. I left the hospital with all my parts. Such are the trials and tribulations of war.

Over my many years of service in the army, not once did I have to go to a doctor for help. But later, my wounds forced me to. It was 1948. I was a student at Frunze Academy. We were conducting marching practice for the parade on Red Square. It was physically very demanding and resulted in the opening of the wound on my right leg. Several tiny pieces of Matilda armor had worked their way out. And my left leg had swollen considerably. The medical conclusion was that I should be excused from all marching activity for the rest of my student time.

This was the first serious caution: "Remember your foreign-made shrapnel!" It was the beginning of almost forty years of wearing an elastic bandage on my left knee whenever I engaged in any strenuous physical activity.

157

During my annual officer's physical examination, the surgeons persistently recommended that I undergo an operation to remove these fragments from my left leg. But they could not exclude the possibility of unforeseen complications. I had to laugh it off every time, saying: "These fragments are made of high-quality American armor plate. I think everything will be all right!"

And so I held them off for thirty years.

Something unbelievable happened sometime at the end of the 1970s. I was vacationing at a military rest area in Georgia. It was summer, an excellent time for swimming. A storm arose, lasting two days. When the sea had calmed, shifting sand and pebbles were obstructing the beach. Many of the vacationers, including myself, helped the staff of the sanitorium to clean the driftwood and debris from the beach. Before doing this, I should have gone back to my room for the elastic bandage. But I was lazy. Why bother.

While I was working, I did not forget about my wounded left leg. I tried to shift all the weight of the load to my right lower leg. The result was excruciating pain. The next day, I could not get my leg into my pants. Three days of bed rest. This calamity befell me a week before the end of my vacation. I made it home with great difficulty. The doctors there decided to wait for the swelling to go down, then discuss the issue of hospitalization and surgery.

As they say, "it's an ill wind that blows nobody good." The swelling went down, and I again refused to be hospitalized. I have not regretted that decision to this day.

Almost twenty years have passed without any recurrence, despite any stresses I put on my leg: I drive a car and work the garden at my dacha. I have thrown the elastic bandage away. I do not limit my physical activities. The doctors think that the large (Sherman) fragment under my left kneecap has displaced. I can dress and undress easier. And now, there is nothing pinching in my leg. It would be pointless to probe around [for the shrapnel piece]. What a relief!

With the years, more and more often my wounds ache in bad weather. My fellow *Emchist* Gevorg Chobanyan, himself seriously wounded, calms me, and himself at the same time, with the words: "Can't sleep? Do your wounds bother you at night? They are your wounds. Accept your fate! These veteran pieces of foreign shrapnel will go with you to another world!"

Notes

About the Author

1. The Order of Lenin, instituted on 6 April 1930, was the highest civilian award that could be bestowed by the Soviet government, in connection with high achievement in the social and political field. The Order of the Red Banner, instituted on 1 August 1924, was a high combat award bestowed for the accomplishment of a particularly dangerous feat in which there was clear risk to life. The Order of Alexander Nevskiy, instituted on 29 July 1942, was bestowed on commanders down to platoon level for display of personal bravery or skillful command that ensured the success of a combat operation. The Order of the Patriotic War, instituted on 20 May 1942, was awarded to military personnel and partisans whose courage and bravery led to the success of combat operations. The 1st degree award was in red enamel and gold and the 2d degree in red enamel and silver. The Order of the Red Star, instituted on 6 April 1930, was awarded to persons of all ranks for courage and resoluteness in battle, outstanding organization, and skillful leadership of combat actions, as a result of which the enemy suffered a significant loss.

Translator's Introduction

1. Many accounts describe the Lend-Lease program to the Soviet Union. See, for example, Edward R. Stettinius Jr., *Lend-Lease: Weapon for Victory* (New York: Macmillan, 1944); T. H. Vail Motter, *The Persian Corridor and Aid to Russia* (Washington DC: Government Printing Office, 1952); Robert Huhn Jones, *The Roads to Russia: United States Lend-Lease to the Soviet Union* (Norman: University of Oklahoma Press, 1969); and Hubert Paul Van Tuyll, "Lend-Lease and the Great Patriotic War, 1941–1945" (Ph.D. dissertation, Texas A & M University, 1986).

2. *Sovetskaya voyennaya entsiklopediya* [Soviet military encyclopedia], vol. 4 (Moscow: Voyenizdat, 1977), s.v. *Lend-liz* [Lend-lease], p. 599.

3. This recent Soviet perspective is found in the article by A. S.

Orlov and V. P. Kozhanov, "Lend-liz: Vzglyad Cherez Polveka" [Lend-lease, A glance across a half-century], in *Novaya i noveyshaya istoriya*, no. 3 (1994), pp. 176–94. See Boris V. Sokolov, "The Role of Lend-Lease in Soviet Military Efforts, 1941–1945," *Journal of Slavic Military Studies* 7, no. 3 (September 1994), pp. 567–86, quote on p. 581. By definition, the Great Patriotic War is the conflict that occurred between the USSR and Germany from 22 June 1941 to 9 May 1945. World War II is the larger, global conflict that began with Germany's invasion of Poland in September 1939 and ended with Japan's surrender in September 1945.

4. For a description of this power plant, see R. P. Hunnicutt, *Sherman: A History of the American Medium Tank* (Novato CA: Presidio, 1978), p. 74.

5. *Correspondence between the Chairman of the Council of Ministers of the USSR and the Presidents of the USA and the Prime Ministers of Great Britain during the Great Patriotic War of 1941–1945* (Moscow: Foreign Languages Publishing House, 1957), 2:30. Stalin's letter was dated 18 July 1942; it expressed the opinion that Soviet experts considered the diesel motor best for tanks.

6. For more details on the organization of Soviet armor units and their employment in combat, see *Red Armor Combat Orders: Combat Regulations for Tank and Mechanized Forces, 1944*, trans. Joseph G. Welsh, ed. Richard N. Armstrong (London: Frank Cass, 1991).

7. The closest equivalent to "guards" designation in the system of the American armed forces is a Presidential Unit Citation. This award, represented by a gold-framed blue ribbon, is granted to a unit by declaration of the president of the United States and becomes a permanent award for the unit and any person assigned to the unit at the time the combat action occurred for which the citation was awarded. In a similar fashion, Soviet military units designated as "guards" units were honored with the addition of the word "guards" to the unit name and banner, the word "guards" to the rank of every soldier, and a "guards" badge on every soldier's tunic pocket.

8. See the chapter entitled "His Majesty, the Azimuth."

Author's Introduction

1. In Russian, *tankist-inomarochnik*. The second word is compounded from *innostrannaya marka*, meaning foreign design or brand. The plural of this is *inomarochniki*.

2. The *panzerfaust* was a shoulder-fired antitank rocket launcher that fired a shaped-charge warhead.

3. In Soviet military terminology, a *front* was a large formation, roughly equivalent to an American or British army group. It was generally commanded by an officer in the rank of army general or marshal and normally was subordinated to the Supreme High Command in Moscow, which exercised its command authority through *Stavka*.

4. The Order of Glory was instituted on 8 November 1943 as an award to privates and sergeants of the Red Army and junior lieutenants in aviation who displayed bravery, courage, and selflessness in combat. The order had three degrees, and thus after receiving the third award of this order, the recipient was named a "full holder" of the Order of Glory.

The First Difficult Trials

1. When referring to land through which a major river flows, Europeans, including Russians, use the terms "right" and "left" bank. The right bank is to the right when one's back is toward the river's source. In the case of Ukraine, the Dnieper River flows generally south, so the right bank would be those lands that lie on the west bank of the river. To cite an analogous example in the United States, Missouri is on the right bank of the Mississippi River, and Illinois is on the left bank.

2. The Second Ukrainian *Front* was created on 20 October 1943 by renaming the Steppe *Front*. It was composed of three guards armies, four combined arms armies, a guards tank army, and an air army. The Danube River Flotilla, an assemblage of vessels and forces that constituted a riverine force, was also subordinated to the *front*. During the period from October to December 1943, the Second Ukrainian *Front* was conducting an operation to enlarge the bridgehead that had been captured in right-bank Ukraine, from Kremenchug to Dnepropetrovsk.

3. Some tanks of this era, the T-34 among them, had neutral steer capability, i.e., with the transmission in neutral, with a push of the steering bar in either direction, the driver could cause one track to go forward and the other backward, turning the vehicle around on its own axis. The Sherman could turn only by moving forward or backward and holding one track.

4. The crew position of driver in a Soviet tank was called driver-

mechanic because this soldier was also responsible for all operator-level maintenance on the automotive systems of the tank.

5. A track thrown to the inside was dislodged from some or all of the road wheels toward the vehicle's hull. Conversely, a track thrown to the outside was dislodged away from the vehicle's hull. In either case, to effect repair the track normally had to be broken (separated), remounted to the road wheels, and rejoined, a procedure that under the best conditions could not be accomplished in less than thirty minutes.

Rain, Snow, and Mud

1. By table of organization, a tank brigade was made up of battalions. But in a mechanized brigade, a tank regiment comprised three tank companies (DL).

2. Ground pressures (the ratio of a tank's weight to the surface area of its track in ground contact) of tanks employed at this time were as follows (pounds/square inch): Tiger:14.5, Panther:12.0, Ferdinand assault gun:16.2, T-34:11.8, and Sherman:10.2. This is one indicator of the vehicle's capability to traverse soft ground, vehicles having less ground pressure being more capable. Tanks with greater ground pressure, i.e., having a relatively narrower tread width, tend to mire more quickly (DL).

3. Loza uses this word in two forms throughout the text—*desantniki* and *tankodesantniki*. Both are rooted in the word *desant*, as in "descend" or "descent." In military Russian, a *desant* is an assault or attack employing a special means of delivery, such as an airplane (parachute), helicopter, amphibious landing craft, or, in this particular case, the tank. Infantry troops were assigned or attached to the Soviet tank units and rode into battle literally holding onto rails welded to the sides of the tank turrets. When the tanks closed with the enemy, these infantry troops, armed with submachine guns, dismounted and attacked to neutralize enemy infantry and antitank troops.

Friendly Fire

1. "Katyusha" was the common name for the 132-mm truck-mounted multiple rocket launcher. After mid-1943, these systems were mounted primarily on American trucks.

2. This weapon system was designed to fire indirectly, like artillery or mortars. The language of the original Russian text supports

the inference that the systems were laid and fired directly over the truck cabs at the position of the two Sherman tanks.

3. Just as American soldiers called the Germans "Jerry," Soviet soldiers called him "Fritz."

Darkness and Wind

1. This included shovels, axes, mattocks, and tankers' bars.

A "Cocktail" for the Shermans

1. The Soviets always calculated the correlation of forces before commencing any large-scale operation to ensure that they had amassed sufficient densities of principal weapons and troops to achieve victory over the enemy. These densities were expressed in ratios.

2. *Pistolet-pulemet Shpagina* (submachine gun of the Shpagin design), 7.62 mm, with 71-round drum magazine. This weapon was accepted for issue to the Soviet Armed Forces on 21 December 1940 but is commonly referred to as the *ppsh-41*.

An Unbelievable Event

1. This is a canvas bag attached to the side of the main gun that collects the spent cartridges from the coaxially mounted .30 caliber machine gun.

2. This also would have been an American vehicle.

A Daring Raid

1. All branches of the Russian military services use the term *yazyk*, literally "tongue," to denote a prisoner captured for the specific purpose of gaining intelligence through interrogation.

Know Your Azimuth!

1. The Budapest operation, an offensive fought by forces of the Second Ukrainian *Front*, commanded by Marshal Malinovskiy, and the Third Ukrainian *Front*, commanded by Marshal Tolbukhin, lasted from 29 October 1944 to 13 February 1945. The Soviet forces were opposed by the German forces of Army Group Center in Czechoslovakia and Army Group South in Hungary. Soviet forces reached the outskirts of Budapest in heavy fighting around 20 December, just as the Germans were launching their counteroffensive in the Ardennes in the west (Battle of the Bulge). At the

conclusion of the operation some three weeks later, Soviet forces had wrested control of Budapest away from the Germans. Like Romania before it, the Hungarian government was forced to abandon its alliance with Germany, opening the way for Soviet forces to advance toward Vienna, the capital of Austria. See *Sovetskaya Voyennaya Entsiklopediya* (Moscow: Voyenizdat, 1976), 1:612–15, s.v. *Budapeshtskaya Operatsiya 1944–45*.

2. *Stavka* was the highest military headquarters in Moscow, which controlled the actions of the *front* commanders.

3. The implication of this sentence is that the other corps in this army was equipped with the Soviet T-34 tank.

Ice Captive

1. *Budapest, Vienna, Prague* (Moscow: Izdatel'stvo "Nauka," 1965), p. 137 (DL).

The Charmed Sherman

1. A maximum number of miles or engine hours, whichever occurred first, was established for the Sherman, upon reaching which the vehicle was to be turned in to higher echelons of maintenance for refurbishing.

A Brief Fight

1. The Vienna operation, conducted by forces of both the Second and Third Ukrainian *Fronts*, lasted from 16 March to 15 April 1945. Its purpose was to defeat German forces in the western portion of Hungary and seize Vienna, the capital of Austria. By mid-April, these goals had been achieved. The Germans in Hungary were defeated, and the eastern portion of Austria and its capital were cleared of German forces. See *Sovetskaya Voyennaya Entsiklopediya* (Moscow: Voyenizdat, 1976), 2:94–96, s.v. *Venskaya Operatsiya 1945*.

2. This is a tactical exploitation of the well-known "accordion effect." Any formation, whether it be men or machines, tends to expand upon starting movement and compress upon halting movement.

3. Central Archive of the Ministry of Defense, 6GTA Collection, index 367293, item 2, sheet 16; Collection 240, index 16400, item 4, sheets 84–85 (DL).

Racing Like a Whirlwind

1. A bounding antipersonnel mine had a small charge that propelled the mine upward out of the ground, after which the mine detonated, spraying shrapnel outward horizontally. Conventional antipersonnel mines, in contrast, detonated in the ground, spraying shrapnel upward. Of the two, bounding antipersonnel mines were much the deadlier against personnel.

Give Us Smoke!

1. Order No. 081, 8 April 1944, of the Supreme High Command awarded the name "Dnestrovskaya" to the 233d Tank Brigade. (DL) [This is an honorific title, denoting combat achievement of a unit.]

Greetings, Emcha

1. The wartime food rationing system in the Soviet Union provided for varying levels of caloric content for every citizen of the USSR, depending on their location and vocation. This included members of the armed forces. Soldiers at the front were allocated a higher daily caloric intake than were soldiers in training or deployed in rear areas.

On the Eve

1. For a description of this operation in English, see David M. Glantz, *Leavenworth Papers No. 7, August Storm: The Soviet 1945 Strategic Offensive in Manchuria,* and *No. 8, August Storm: Soviet Tactical and Operational Combat in Manchuria, 1945* (Fort Leavenworth: Combat Studies Institute, 1983).

2. *Informburo* was the Soviet government's official source for release of news inside the USSR during the war.

3. Loza does not mention anywhere how his father came to be a Red Army private. In all likelihood, he was subject to conscription by his age and physical condition but fortunate to be employed in his civilian specialty, despite being assigned to an infantry unit.

A Leap across the Desert

1. Then, as now, gauges in the driver's compartment were marked with bands of green, yellow, and red for quick reference.

2. All Soviet tanks also carried a length of log, which, when rigged to the tracks with the tow cables, enabled the tank to recover itself.

Grand Khingan

1. According to the author, from the end of 1945 through 1948 the Soviet Army consumed a great quantity of captured Japanese food stocks that it had removed from Manchuria, including large amounts of *gaolyan* and *chumiza* that were used to make *kasha* (porridge). Letter from author to translator, 16 June 1995.

Mukden

1. We *inomarochniki* of the 9th Guards Mechanized Corps were not permitted to go to Port Arthur and Dal'nya for political reasons. This was decided by the higher leadership (both in the army and *front* and perhaps in Moscow)—in the Kremlin office of the Supreme High Command. The leadership decided that the "disgrace of the defeat of tsarist Russia in 1905 had to be erased by domestic, and not by lend-lease, weapons, least of all tanks." Although almost all the wheeled transportation of the 5th Guards Stalingrad Tank Corps was of Lend-Lease origin—Studebaker, Ford, and Willys—the principal combat vehicles—the T-34 tanks—were Soviet. (DL)

2. The Russian here is *smertnik*, or one who is condemned to death. The implication is that the Japanese would have formed squads of suicidal soldiers, willing to engage the Soviet tanks with explosives carried on their bodies.

3. By instruction of the People's Commissariat of Defense, each combatant at the front received a daily ration of one hundred grams of vodka. (DL)

Epilogue

1. The Matilda was a twenty-six-ton British-designed tank of the late 1930s, armed with a 40-mm cannon and intended for an infantry support role. From the moment of his first assignment to a foreign-manufactured tank, Loza's officer identification documents were overstampped *inomarochnik*, and a similar annotation was made in his personnel file. This ensured that henceforth he would always be assigned to units equipped with foreign equipment. This officer personnel management policy was strictly enforced at all levels and provided for special management of all officers who had experience with foreign equipment. Letter from author to translator, 18 July 1995.

Index

air attacks: German, 49–50, 62–
63, 88, 100; Japanese, 145;
threat of, 93, 136, 144
air-to-air combat, 100
alcohol, consumption of: champagne, 102; medicinal alcohol,
151; vodka, 150, 166 n.3; whiskey, 42; wine, 73
antitank guns, German: concealment for, 14; destroyed in
combat, 33, 103; fields of fire,
11, 28; integration in defense,
70, 78; preparing to fire, 14;
run over by Shermans, 23;
unable to unlimber, 83; use in
built-up areas, 93, 95–96
Austria: burial site of Soviet
soldiers, 38; Loza wounded in,
108, 113, 157; urban combat
in Vienna described, 90–104;
Vienna operation (overview),
90–91
azimuth, maintaining: 64–70,
114–15, 124, 128

Berlin operation, 120
bounty for enemy vehicles, 105
Budapest operation, 163 n.1

chief mechanic, battalion, 3, 4–5
chief of armaments, battalion:
Ivan Korchak, 54, 74, 136–37;
Dmitriy Loza, 9

chief of finance services, battalion, 103–4
chief of staff, battalion: Nikolay
Bogdanov, 56–57, 59–60, 101,
129, 148; in commanders'
reconnaissance group, 123;
consultation with commander,
129; Dmitriy Loza, 52; monitoring column azimuth, 128;
in parliamentary group, 148;
turret frozen, 74
commanders' reconnaissance,
66, 117, 123–24
communications chief, battalion,
53
currency exchange, 103–4
Czechoslovakia: brigade entry
into Šahy, 64; brigade location
in May 1945, 108; burial site of
Soviet soldiers, 38; location of
front line, 61; tactical combat
in, 65–71

deputy commander for maintenance, battalion, 3, 5, 75, 79,
129
deputy commander for maintenance, brigade, 76
desantniki (tankodesantniki):
azimuth written on sub-
machine gun stocks, 66;
dismounted combat role
described, 14–15, 18, 21, 26,

167

phosphorus markers, 127; red rocket, 15, 100. *See also* signal devices

radio communications: brigade net described, 63, 68; command of subordinate elements, 13, 97–98; communication with pilot, 100; monitoring of subordinates' conversations, 98; radio silence, 20, 56, 60, 127; reception of news broadcast, 52–53; report to higher commander, 32, 63, 94; warning of enemy approach, 83
railroads, use of: for delivery of new equipment, 41; embankment used for tank movement, 143–47; German, 83; movement of combat unit to *front*, 4–5; returning tanks to Far East port, 152; transcontinental movement, 111, 126
recovery: battle-damaged tank, 97; captured German vehicle, 59–60; mired tank, 26, 129; overturned tanks, 5; recovery vehicles, 135–36; self-recovery, 130, 133, 165 n.2
road march: on icy roads, 6–7; mission to conduct, 6, 76; night, 66, 73
Romania: burial site for Soviet soldiers, 38; departure from war, 43; fuel mixture named for, 48; German defenses in, 44; mountains compared to Manchuria, 134; reminiscence about, 125; Soviet forces reach,

25, 38; Soviet strategic plan in, 44–45; summer 1944 heat in, 51; tactical combat in, 47

sappers: attachment to battalion, 89; bridge construction, 138–39; guiding tanks through minefields, 67; lack of, on tanks, 88; preparation of march route, 66, 132, 135–36, 137; reinforcement by tank crewmen, 137; tank armies reinforced by, 9
self-propelled gun (German): capture of, 58–59; engagement of, 82–83, 86; sighting of, 70; strength in, 65. *See also* Ferdinand
self-propelled gun (Soviet): carrying submachine gunners, 26; commander's reserve, 98; employment in urban area (Vienna), 92, 94–96, 98–101, 145; sau defined, 92; Soviet strength in, 44, 91, 120; versus German tank, 99
Sherman tank: battle damage to, 12, 32, 48, 69, 78, 79, 85, 93–94, 95, 96, 98, 106, 108, 145; combat in built-up area, 14, 23, 86–87, 91–103; combat losses, 33, 58, 69, 80, 81, 88, 93, 98, 103; comparisons to German tanks, 18–19, 96, 106; comparisons to T-34, 4, 7, 51, 65, 143, 161 n.3, 162 n.2; demilitarization of, 153–55; factory representative, 7–8, 41–42; forest trail, 81–82; ground pressure of, 12, 17–18, 56, 60, 162 n.3; headlights,

of tank from fender, 73, 128;
reaction to air attack, 49–50;
receiving instruction, 5, 35;
receiving new tanks, 112–13
tankodesantniki. See *desantniki*

Ukraine: icy roads, 135; strategic
offensive operation, 24–25;

weather and terrain, 6, 8
Umansk-Batoshansk operation:
overview, 24–25

Vienna operation: overview, 80,
90–91, 164 n.1

Willys, 166 n.1

CPSIA information can be obtained
at www.ICGtesting.com
Printed in the USA
LVOW11*0225300118
564440LV00007BA/96/P